THE BEST POEMS OF 1922

The BEST POEMS
of 1922

Selected
by THOMAS MOULT &

Decorated by
PHILIP HAGREEN

Granger Poetry Library

GRANGER BOOK CO., INC.
GREAT NECK, N.Y.

FIRST PUBLISHED 1923
REPRINTED 1979

INTERNATIONAL STANDARD BOOK NUMBER 0-89609-140-6

LIBRARY OF CONGRESS CATALOG NUMBER 78-74821

PRINTED IN THE UNITED STATES OF AMERICA

To
THE MEMORY
of
ALICE MEYNELL

Contents

(An asterisk denotes America)

(vii)

(ix)

(x)

OF THE ABOVE POEMS several have appeared or are about to appear in volumes restricted to their author's own work. The following publishers are therefore offered the compiler's thanks for their additional permissions :—Burns & Oats : 'The Poet and His Book,' by Alice Meynell. R. Cobden-Sanderson : 'Love in Old Age,' by W. Force Stead. Golden Cockerell Press : 'The Young Man under the Walnut-Tree,' by A. E. Coppard; 'Poets, Painters, and Puddings,' by Richard Hughes. Harcourt Brace & Co. : 'Blue Water,' by John Gould Fletcher; 'Heliodora,' by H. D.; 'Windflower Leaf' and 'Moon-Riders,' by Carl Sandburg; 'Waters of Babylon,' by Louis Untermeyer. William Heinemann : 'Mirror, Mirror,' by R. Graves ; 'Leda,' by Muriel Stuart. Macmillan & Co. : 'The Poor Girl's Meditation,' by P. Colum; 'An Ancient to Ancients,' by T. Hardy ; 'Green Weeds,' by James Stephens. Frederick A. Stokes Co. : 'Song Nets,' from 'Shoes of the Wind,' by Hilda Conkling.

INTRODUCTION

I

'LA BELLE DAME SANS MERCI,' by John Keats, was first printed in a periodical. Readers to whom for various reasons Leigh Hunt's 'Indicator' was inaccessible were thus deprived of a poem which, as the late Mr. Buxton Forman claimed, had profoundly influenced English poetic literature for nearly a century, and which Sir Sidney Colvin has characterized as a classic of the language. Not until twenty-eight years afterwards was 'La Belle Dame sans Merci' republished, and even then it was a slightly different version that Lord Houghton included among Keats's Literary Remains.

The compiler of 'The Best Poems of 1922' desires nothing better than that the circumstances attending the publication of 'the wondrous "Belle Dame"' should be accepted as his justification for adding what may loosely be termed an anthology to the numbers lately issued. By recalling those circumstances he has, however, no intention of flattering the period which is covered by the present volume. But the risk to the poet and his poetry of publication in a periodical remains, although the responsibility is to be attributed neither to periodical nor reader. An article of faith by which this volume has been compiled is that (outside the men of high and declared rank) a majority of those now writing verse—all, that is, who find stimulation in the ownership of a certain degree of imagination and a relative technical standard—are producing and publishing worthy poetry. It is natural that they should desire their successes to be made more widely known, and maybe made permanent, by a less localized and less ephemeral publication than had been originally secured in the magazines and reviews. But they cannot hope that the reading public will be persuaded to search through their hundred pages of collected verse in the hope of encountering two or three good poems as a consequence. Thus republication in book form is very often the private affair of the poet, his publisher, and his own circle.

By emphasizing superior achievement through a different form of volume-publication, in a collection of the best poetry of the particular year in which a successful poem happens to be printed, seems the simplest and most helpful way out of a difficulty which is the cause of mortification to poets and to the reader who desires to be made acquainted with the best poetry of his time. That alongside the work of those whose distinction is greater than their fame should be placed the work of poets of fame as well as distinction—for these, too, are accustomed to make use of the periodicals —is an additional profit accruing mainly, it need hardly be stated, to the poets who find themselves in very distinguished company, and to the reader.

It may be said here that if we were living in an ideal condition for poetry—that is, with readers as eager and ready to make sacrifices for the art as are

the poets themselves—any resemblance to the
accepted form of anthology which this book might
possess would not have existed. For it is intended
primarily to be a *survey* of poetry published in
English and American periodicals as distinct from
volumes, during the twelve months from January
to December, 1922 ; a sort of latter-day ' Indi-
cator,' whose whole purpose might have been to
direct readers to the published poetry deemed
worthy of their attention by the simple process of
recording that on such a date to this or that maga-
zine or journal Mr. So-and-so contributed verses
entitled Such-and-such ; and other poems would
be emphasized in like manner. With every reason
to believe that readers would require no further
persuasion to hunt up for themselves the files of
the periodicals named, the survey would end at
that point. Unfortunately the actual time de-
manded from the reader by the pursuit of this
method would present difficulties, apart alto-
gether from the question of opportunity and
inclination. Therefore, if only for poetry's sake,
the poems must have the additional emphasis of
reproduction.

II

The reprinting of the poems in full being there-
fore necessary, as we have seen, it now remains to
be placed on record that, with hardly an excep-
tion, the various author's have willingly relieved
the compiler of the conventional anthologist's

difficulties. His warmest thanks are offered in return to each of those whose contributions to the year's periodicals have been harvested, especially to several whom it might seem invidious to mention by name, for what must have amounted to real sacrifice on their part ; and to Mr. Wilfred Meynell for permitting the inclusion of a poem by the late Mrs. Meynell, to whose memory it has been thought fitting, reverently and gratefully, to dedicate the complete volume.

To offer thanks to the editors of the various journals in which the poems first appeared, for their ready permissions and wholehearted encouragement, is a duty just as pleasant. A cheering feature of the year, indeed, is the manner in which more and more editors have recognized that the art which is England's chief claim to glory still deserves the encouragement that they are able to give, while in the United States nearly a score of magazines exist exclusively for the publication of verse. Several of these inspire genuine admiration in English readers. Some American daily newspapers publish poetic contributions regularly, although their comparative standards are not necessarily to be gathered from the index to contents in the present book.

The selection of ' The Best Poems of 1922 ' has in no way been prejudiced by the fact that several of the compiler's preferences have been reissued already in books apart from anthologies. But the instances are few—a dozen in all—and no difficulties have been raised as a consequence. To the list of those who are entitled to acknowledgment for favours granted must therefore be added certain publishers whose names have been tabulated at the end of the list of contents.

The order in which the poems are printed is not intended as an indication of their comparative excellence. As will be seen from the list, where the necessary information as to periodical publication has accompanied the title of each poem, the arrangement is strictly chronological. There is a certain sad gratification to be derived from the coincidence by which Mr. de la Mare's beautiful tribute to the late Katherine Mansfield, written and printed while she was still living and working, is the first poem of the book ; for Miss Mansfield was herself a poet as well as a master of the art of the short story. . . .

III

Over all the difficulties inseparable from such a book as ' The Best Poems of 1922 ' the compiler is only too conscious that he has not triumphed. That he was entitled to face them he himself would not admit had any of the students better qualified than he been ready to undertake what is obviously a gigantic task, ill or well done. All he is able to claim, now that several thousand issues of periodicals and a proportionate number of poems have been examined, is that each of the hundred pieces harvested has moved him in the way he believes true poetry should move its audience, and that

each possesses the required character. The title of
the volume is, of course, arbitrary; just as is the
rule by which, through physical limitations, have
been excluded poems of such length as 'Avenal
Gray,' by Mr. Edwin Arlington Robinson (*Poetry*,
Chicago, October); 'Ryton Firs,' by Mr. Las-
celles Abercrombie (the *Chapbook*, London,
February); 'The White Stallion,' by Mr. F. V.
Branford (*English Review*, London, May); and
'The Waste Land,' by Mr. T. S. Eliot (the *Criterion*,
London, October); and doubtless another harvester
would have garnered differently.

But apart from the actual selection the same
general conclusion would doubtless have been
arrived at, however different the policy dictating
the compiler's labour. That, at least, may be said
with assurance, for poets of fame and distinction
in two countries are plainly writing with as much
truth, beauty, and strength as ever they have done,
and poets whose distinction is in no way propor-
tionate to their fame have seldom written better. It
is a matter for pride that the poets of England and
of America have here been assembled together for
perhaps the first time in literary history (at all
events, so far as English publication is concerned)
in a manner that gives the reader no guide to their
nationality except what is revealed by the work
itself. How and in what ways that work may be
different if produced on one or the other side of
the Atlantic will, the compiler believes, be well
worth studying. And if readers in America accept
this opportunity of surveying contemporary

poetry in England, and English readers be persuaded to take a wider interest in American poetry, then the desire that the present compilation might be the first of a series of annual volumes will have additional justification.

THOMAS MOULT

WALTER DE LA MARE
(To Katherine Mansfield)

HORSE IN A FIELD

*'And there was a Horse in the King's Stables ; and the
name of the Horse was Genius.'*—ARABIAN NIGHTS.

WE sat and talked. It was June, and the summer
    light
Lay fair upon ceiling and wall as the day took flight.
Tranquil the room—with its colours and shadows
    wan,
Cherries, and china, and flowers : and the hour slid
    on.
Dark hair, dark eyes, slim fingers—you made the tea,
Pausing with spoon uplifted, to speak to me.
Lulled by our thoughts and our voices, happy were
    we !

And musing, an old, old riddle crept into my head,
' Supposing I just say " Horse in a field," ' I said,
' What do you *see* ?' And we each made answer : ' I,
A roan, long tail, and a red-brick house, near by.'
' I—an old cart-horse and rain !' ' Oh no, not rain :
A mare with a long-legged foal by a pond—oh,
    plain !'
' And I—a hedge—and an elm—and the shadowy
    green
Sloping gently up to the blue, to the West, I
    mean.' . . .

And now. On the field that I see night's darkness
    lies.
A brook brawls near : there are stars in the empty
    skies.
The grass is deep : and dense, as I push my way,
From sour-nettled ditch sweeps fragrance of cluster-
    ing may.
I come to a stile. And lo, on the further side,
Beneath still, umbrageous, night-black fronds,
    spread wide,
A giant cedar broods. . . . And in crescent's gleam—
A horse, milk-pale, sleek-shouldered, strange as a
    dream,

Startled, it lifts its muzzle, deep eyes agaze,
With silk-plaited mane . . .
            ' Whose pastures are thine to graze ?
Creature delicate, lovely, with womanlike head,
Sphinx-like, gazelle-like. . . . Where tarries thy
    rider ? ' I said.
And I scanned by that sinking slip's thin silver shed
A high-pooped saddle of leather, night-darkened
    red,
Stamped with a pattern of gilding ; and over it
    thrown
A cloak, chain-buckled, with one great glamorous
    stone
Wan as the argent moon when o'er fields of wheat
Like Dian she broods, and steals to Endymion's feet.
Interwoven with silver that cloak from seam to seam.
And at toss of the head from its damascened bridle
    did beam

Mysterious glare in the dead of the dark. . . .
                                        ' Thy name,
Fantastical Steed ? And thy pedigree ?
Peace out of Storm, is the tale: or, *Beauty—of Jeopardy?*'

The water weeps. Not a footfall. And midnight here.
Why tarries Darkness's bird ? Spiced and clear
Slopes to yon hill with its stars the moorland sweet.
There sigh the airs of far heaven. And the dreamer's
    feet
Scatter the leagues of paths secret to where at last
    meet
Roads called Wickedness, Righteousness, broad-
    flung or strait,
And a third that leads on to the Queen of fair Elf-
    land's gate.

This then the horse that I see : swift as the wind ;
That none may master or mount ; and none may
    bind ;
But she, his Mistress ; cloaked, and at throat that
    gem—
Dark head, dark eyes, slim shoulder . . .
            God speed, K. M.

JAMES STEPHENS

GREEN WEEDS

TO be not jealous give not love :
Rate not thy fair all fair above,
Or thou'lt be decked in green, the hue
That jealousy is bounden to.

That lily hand, those lips of fire,
Those dewy eyes that spill desire,
Those mounds of lambent snow, may be
Found anywhere it pleaseth thee

To turn : then turn, and be not mad
Tho' all of loveliness she had :
She hath not all of loveliness ;
A store remains wherewith to bless

The bee, the bird, the butterfly,
And thou—go, search with those that fly
For that which thou shalt easy find
On every path and any wind.

Nor dream that she is Seal and Star
Who is but as her sisters are,
And whose reply is yes and no
To all that come and all that go.

'I love——' Then, love again, my friend,
Enjoy thy love without an end :
'I love——' Ah, cease ! know what is what !
Thou dost not love if she love not.

For, if thou truly loved her,
From thee away she would not ſtir,
But ever at thy side would be
Thyself and thy felicity.

Go, drape thee in the greeny hue ;
Thou art not Love ; she is not True,
And no more need be said—adieu.

CARL SANDBURG

THE flower is repeated
out of old winds, out of
old tunes.

The wind repeats these, it
muſt have these, over and
over again.

Oh, windflowers so fresh,
Oh, beautiful leaves, here
now again.

The domes over
fall to pieces.
The ſtones under
fall to pieces.
Rain and ice
wreck the works.
The wind keeps, the windflowers
keep, the leaves laſt,
The wind young and ſtrong lets
these laſt longer than ſtones.

ALFRED PERCEVAL GRAVES

UISEÓ MO LEANB

(*After the Gaelic*)

SHOHEEN, shoho ! my child is my treasure,
  My sparkling jewel, my share of the world.
Shoheen, shoho ! how great is the pleasure
  When in your soft bed you lie happily curled.
O child of my bosom, may slumber go well with you,
  Joy and Good Fortune walk ever your way ;
God's little Son and His Nurse come to dwell with
    you !
  So go to sleep without start till the day !

On Slieve na Shee the Fairies are shining,
  Among the moonbeams in circles they sport.
'Tis eastward now their host is inclining
  To win my bright babe to their wonderful fort.
I call you, my heart, do not let them misguide you
  By song or by dance or sweet shaken bell-bough.
Am I not praying against them beside you ?
  So husho ! my baby, hark not to them now.

Above your bed your bright angel keeper
  Looks sweet and gentle down into your face ;
To Heaven he'd bear my own little sleeper,
  For with you he'd think it a happier place.
Lie down then, lie down then, my beautiful treasure,
  Since here with your mother you still must abide,
For God does not grudge me my play and my plea-
    sure
  My Heaven upon Earth at my happy one's side.

ROBERT FROST

(*Circa*, 1922)

I STAID the night for shelter at a farm
Behind the mountain, with a mother and son,
Two old-believers. They did all the talking.

The Mother.
   Folks think a witch who has familiar spirits
   She *could* call up to pass a winter evening,
   But *won't,* should be burned at the stake or some-
      thing.
   Summoning spirits isn't ' Button, button,
   Who's got the button?' you're to understand.

The Son.
   Mother can make a common table rear
   And kick with two legs like an army mule.

The Mother.
   And when I've done it, what good have I done?
   Rather than tip a table for you, let me
   Tell you what Ralle the Sioux Control once told
      me.
   He said the dead had souls, but when I asked him
   How that could be—I thought the dead were souls,
   He broke my trance. Don't that make you sus-
      picious
   That there's something the dead are keeping back?
   Yes, there's something the dead are keeping back.

The Son.
> You wouldn't want to tell him what we have
> Up attic, mother?

The Mother.
> Bones—a skeleton.

The Son.
> But the headboard of mother's bed is pushed
> Against the attic door : the door is nailed.
> It's harmless. Mother hears it in the night
> Halting perplexed behind the barrier
> Of door and headboard. Where it wants to get
> Is back into the cellar where it came from.

The Mother.
> We'll never let them, will we, son? We'll never!

The Son.
> It left the cellar forty years ago
> And carried itself like a pile of dishes
> Up one flight from the cellar to the kitchen,
> Another from the kitchen to the bedroom,
> Another from the bedroom to the attic
> Right past both father and mother, and neither
>   stopped it.
> Father had gone upstairs ; mother was downstairs.
> I was a baby : I don't know where I was.

The Mother.
> The only fault my husband found with me—
> I went to sleep before I went to bed,
> Especially in winter when the bed

Might just as well be ice and the clothes snow.
The night the bones came up the cellar-stairs
Toffile had gone to bed alone and left me,
But left an open door to cool the room off
So as to sort of turn me out of it.
I was just coming to myself enough
To wonder where the cold was coming from,
When I heard Toffile upstairs in the bedroom
And thought I heard him downstairs in the cellar.
The board we had laid down to walk dry-shod on
When there was water in the cellar in spring
Struck the hard cellar bottom. And then someone
Began the stairs, two footsteps for each step,
The way a man with one leg and a crutch,
Or little child, comes up. It wasn't Toffile :
It wasn't any one who could be there.
The bulkhead double-doors were double-locked
And swollen tight and buried under snow.
The cellar windows were banked up with sawdust
And swollen tight and buried under snow.
It was the bones. I knew them—and good reason.
My first impulse was to get to the knob
And hold the door. But the bones didn't try
The door ; they halted helpless on the landing,
Waiting for things to happen in their favour.
The faintest restless rustling ran all through them.
I never could have done the thing I did
If the wish hadn't been too strong in me
To see how they were mounted for this walk.
I had a vision of them put together
Not like a man, but like a chandelier.
So suddenly I flung the door wide on him.

A moment he stood balancing with emotion,
And all but lost himself. (A tongue of fire
Flashed out and licked along his upper teeth.
Smoke rolled inside the sockets of his eyes.)
Then he came at me with one hand outstretched,
The way he did in life once ; but this time
I struck the hand off brittle on the floor,
And fell back from him on the floor myself.
The finger-pieces slid in all directions.
(Where did I see one of those pieces lately ?
Hand me my button-box—it must be there.)

I sat up on the floor and shouted, ' Toffile,
It's coming up to you.' It had its choice
Of the door to the cellar or the hall.
It took the hall door for the novelty,
And set off briskly for so slow a thing,
Still going every which way in the joints, though,
So that it looked like lightning or a scribble,
From the slap I had just now given its hand.
I listened till it almost climbed the stairs
From the hall to the only finished bedroom,
Before I got up to do anything ;
Then ran and shouted, ' Shut the bedroom door,
Toffile, for my sake ! ' ' Company,' he said,
' Don't make me get up ; I'm too warm in bed.'
So lying forward weakly on the handrail
I pushed myself upstairs, and in the light
(The kitchen had been dark) I had to own
I could see nothing. ' Toffile, I don't see it.
It's with us in the room, though. It's the bones.'
' What bones ? ' ' The cellar bones—out of the grave.'

That made him throw his bare legs out of bed
And sit up by me and take hold of me.
I wanted to put out the light and see
If I could see it, or else mow the room,
With our arms at the level of our knees,
And bring the chalk-pile down. 'I'll tell you
        what—
It's looking for another door to try.
The uncommonly deep snow has made him think
Of his old song, *The Wild Colonial Boy,*
He always used to sing along the tote-road.
He's after an open door to get out-doors.
Let's trap him with an open door up attic.'
Toffile agreed to that, and sure enough,
Almost the moment he was given an opening,
The steps began to climb the attic stairs.
I heard them. Toffile didn't seem to hear them.
'Quick,' I slammed to the door and held the knob.
' Toffile, get nails.' I made him nail the door shut,
And push the headboard of the bed against it.

Then we asked was there anything
Up attic that we'd ever want again.
The attic was less to us than the cellar.
If the bones liked the attic, let them like it,
Let them *stay* in the attic. When they sometimes
Come down the stairs at night and stand perplexed
Behind the door and headboard of the bed,
Brushing their chalky skull with chalky fingers,
With sounds like the dry rattling of a shutter,
That's what I sit up in the dark to say—
To no one any more since Toffile died.

Let them stay in the attic since they went there.
I promised Toffile to be cruel to them
For helping them be cruel once to him.

The Son.
  We think they had a grave down in the cellar.

The Mother.
  We know they had a grave down in the cellar.

The Son.
  We never could find out whose bones they were.

The Mother
  Yes, we could too, son. Tell the truth for once.
  They were a man's his father killed for me.
  I mean a man he killed instead of me.
  The least I could do was help dig their grave.
  We were about it one night in the cellar.
  Son knows the story : but 'twas not for him
  To tell the truth, suppose the time had come.
  Son looks surprised to see me end a lie
  We'd kept up all these years between ourselves
  So as to have it ready for outsiders.
  But to-night I don't care enough to lie—
  I don't remember why I ever cared.
  Toffile, if he were here, I don't believe
  Could tell you why he ever cared himself. . . .

  She hadn't found the finger-bone she wanted
  Among the buttons poured out in her lap.

  I verified the name next morning : Toffile.
  The rural letter-box said Toffile Barre.

CHARLOTTE MEW

THE RAMBLING SAILOR

IN the old back streets o' Pimlico
On the docks at Monte Video
At the Ring o' Bells on Plymouth Hoe
He'm arter me now wheerever I go.
An' dirty nights when the wind do blow
I can hear him sing-songin' up from sea—:
Oh! no man nor woman's bin friend to me
An' to-day I'm feared wheer to-morrow I'll be,
Sin' the night the moon lay whist and white
On the road goin' down to the Lizard Light
When I heard him hummin' behind me.

'Oh! look, boy, look in your sweetheart's eyes
    So deep as sea an' so blue as skies ;
An' 'tis better to kiss than to chide her,
If they tell 'ee no tales, they'll tell 'ee no lies
        Of the little brown mouse
        That creeps into the house
To lie sleepin' so quiet beside her.

'Oh! hold 'ee long, but hold 'ee light
Your true man's hand when you find him,
He'll help 'ee home on a darksome night
        Wi' a somethin' bright
        That he'm holdin' tight
In the hand that he keeps behind him.

'Oh ! sit 'ee down to your whack o' pies
So hot's the stew and the brew likewise
But whiles you'm scrapin' the plates and dishes,
A'gapin' down in the shiversome sea
For the delicate mossels inside o' we
Theer's a passel o' hungry fishes.'

At the *Halte des Marins* at *Saint Nazaire*
I cussed him, sittin' astride his chair ;
An' Christmas Eve on the Mary Clare
I pitched him a'down the hatch-way stair.
But 'Shoutin' and cloutin's nothin' to me,
Nor the hop nor the skip nor the jump,' says he,
'For I be walkin' on every quay . . .'

'So look, boy, look in the dear maid's eyes
And take the true man's hand,
And eat your fill o' your whack o' pies
Till you'm starin' up wheer the sea-crow flies
Wi' your head lyin' soft in the sand.'

C. HENRY WARREN

NOW IS THE SUNLIGHT MELLOW

NOW is the sunlight mellow and the beech-leaves
Fall to the dank mould and fade and shrivel.
Now in the North comes winter whistling boldly
And the last colours of the day are passing.
To the dark house of memory I've gathered,
Through the long hours, rich store of varied trea-
    sures ;
And now they lie, their loveliness concealing,
Like precious cloths hid in a room of darkness,
Their gold and blue and saffron from all seeing
Shut, save when the miser's meagre candle
Furtively on their gloom a brightness throws.

O, that upon my darkness, swift-revealing,
Would break some light of faith and show a purpose
In this of suffering, and that of laughter,
In all this beauty at the senses knocking,
And all that loveliness so knit with sorrow !
But still to the dank mould the leaves are falling,
Shrill and more shrill the wind in the north whistles
And the last colour of the day has fled.

KATHARINE TYNAN

SHE ASKS FOR NEW EARTH

LORD, when I find at last Thy Paradise,
Be it not all too bright for human eyes,
Lest I go sick for home through the high mirth—
For Thy new Heaven, Lord, give me new earth.

Give of Thy mansions, Lord, a house so small
Where they can come to me who were my all ;
Let them run home to me just as of yore,
Glad to sit down with me and go out no more.

Give me a garden, Lord, and a low hill,
A field and a babbling brook that is not still ;
Give me an orchard, Lord, in leaf and bloom,
And my birds to sing to me in a quiet gloam.

There shall no canker be in leaf or bud,
But glory on hill and sea and the green wood ;
There, there shall none grow old but all be new,
No moth or rust shall fret nor thief break through.

Set Thou a mist upon Thy glorious sun ;
Lest we should faint for night and be undone ;
Give us the high clean wind and the wild rain,
Lest that we faint with thirst and go in pain.

Let there be Winter there and the joy of Spring,
Summer and Autumn and the harvesting ;
Give us all things we loved on earth of old,
Never to slip from out our clinging hold.

Give me a little house for my desire,
The man and the children to sit by my fire,
And friends to be crowding in to our lit hearth—
For Thy new Heaven, Lord, give me new earth !

ROY MELDRUM

CONTRARIA

SOMETIMES the dykes, which lap with wintry
    flood
When every wind is numb at dead of night,
A thousand tapers kindle, and the mud
Of lanes with silver crucibles is bright.
The meanest pool, no bigger than a hand,
Catches Orion's shoulder, as he strides
Over the margin of the frozen land,
And all heaven's magic on the puddle rides.
But if the stars their images refuse,
These waters are a waste of eyeless fear,
A cold obscurity, in which men lose
Trust in themselves, and drift, afraid to steer.
Without the moon there's ruin in the sea,
And with her the least spring has alchemy.

How faint, when winter in swift snow descends,
Is the suspicion of another spring.
When hedges creak with ice, and drear lane-ends
Assemble bird and beast in dismal ring ;
When twilight ever hovers in the air,
Who then can see the blue and burning sky
Where song-birds float, or smell the blossom fair,
Or taste the virtue of the sun's clear eye ?
So when I see a wintry solitude
In long cold distances between us spread,
Upon my spirit drifts of despair intrude,
Like whirling ghosts of sweet remembrance dead.
But yet I know, as often as I'm wise,
That spring sleeps somewhere in thy truthful eyes.

Oft out of humour and grown delicate
With the confinement of that inward cell,
Where passions, dreams, and inbred visions sate
The heart that breeds them, sullen I rebel
From love's soft air and tender subtleties.
Then to the genial plains of earth I go,
Where balsams choice as in the Hesperides,
Upon the morn's cool forehead sweetly blow.
There, as the generous team strains to the trace,
As ridges noiseless swell, as sinews tire,
Disorder to a careless joy gives place,
And heaven lies wondrous near a simple shire.
Then do I find how treacherous earth can be,
My fond escape has led me nigher thee.

Since we are like our vows to disengage,
And close upon farewell, and half afraid
The finger trembles down love's latest page,
One thing I'd say, and leave the rest unsaid.
Pale Egypt crushed between her royal lips
The pearl of Venus ; and the stratagem
Of fairer Helen matched a thousand ships,
And Sheba's riddles wise Jerusalem.
But something thou of Eve, when Eden lost,
She still remembered the nobility
Which shaped her, and with smiles rebuked the cost.
Of all that reassured her memory.
And, had I used it, chance by thee was given,
In a small age to know the space of heaven.

HELEN COALE CREW

IRISH SONG

WHERE the highway steps along
(In Donegal, in Donegal!)
I gave my feet the choice o' way, wherever they
would roam.
They might have marched to Londonderry, Belfast,
Dublin . . .
The foolish, eager feet o' me, they marched straight
home!

A little gown o' blue you wore
(In Donegal, in Donegal !)
Cried out to me, *Come in ! Come in !* Your apron it
said *Stay!*
The tying o' the plaid shawl across the warm heart
o' you
Tied in—along the heart o' me—I couldn't get away.

I took off my wander shoes
(In Donegal, in Donegal !),
The highway stepped along alone, until it slipped
from view.
I laid aside my dusty dreams, hung up my ragged
lifetime,
And rested feet and heart o' me before the sight o'
you !

JOHN DRINKWATER

VOTIVE

O MOON, swung there immeasurably far,
    Yet only in the pear-tree top, how then
Shall we body in thought the beauty that you are—
    Your wizardry upon the souls of men ?

Hush ! Let us say it is the tender light
    That falls in silver circumstance and red
Dimly upon the regions of the night,
    And saying this how little then is said.

Why should this mute enchantment thus possess
    Our hearts in adoration—how should come
This worship of a ghost of quietness,
    Of spectral tides that move not and are dumb ?

Why do we worship ? We are but strays of will,
    While the sun takes us. Folded now and far
From the day's light, we are minds possessed
       and still,
    Vision and peace. We worship what we are.

HAROLD MONRO

FATE

I

I HAVE so often
Examined all this well-known room
That I inhabit.

There is the open window ;
There the locked door, the door I cannot open,
The only doorway.

When at the keyhole often, often
I bend and listen, I can always hear
A muffled conversation.

An argument :
An angry endless argument of people
Who live behind ;

Now loudly talking,
Now dimly to their separate conflict moving
Behind the door.

There they seem prisoned,
As I, in this lone room that I inhabit :
My life ; my body.

You, of the previous being,
You who once made me and who now discuss me,
Tell me your verdict, and I will obey it !

You, long ago,
With doubting hands and eager trembling fingers,
Prepared my room.

Before I came,
Each gave his token for remembrance, brought it,
And then retired behind the bolted door.

There is the pot of honey
One left, and there the jar of vinegar
On the same table.

Who poured that water
Shining beside the flask of yellow wine ?
Who sighed so softly ?

Who brought that living flower to the room ?
Who groaned, that I can ever hear the echo ?
You do not answer.

Meanwhile from out the window
Sounds penetrate of building other houses :
Men building houses.

And so it may be
Some day I'll find some doorway in the wall—
What shall I take them ?

What shall I take them
Beyond those doorways, in the other rooms ?
What shall I bring them,
That they may love me ?

Fatal question !
For all the jangling voices rise together ;
I seem to hear :

'What shall he take them ? ' . . .
Beyond their closed door there's no final answer.
They are debating.

II

O Fate ! Have you no other gift
Than voices in a muffled room ?
Why do you live behind your door,
And hide yourself in angry gloom ?

And why, again, should you not have
One purpose only, one sole word,
Ringing forever round my heart,
Plainly delivered, plainly heard ?

Your conversation fills my brain
And tortures all my life, and yet
Gives no result. I often think
You've grown so old that you forget ;

And having learnt man's fatal trick
Of talking, talking, talking still,
You're tired of definite design,
And laugh at having lost your will.

33

ANNA DE BARY

LONELY, lonely lay the hill,
Not a bird was there to sing,
Not a bee was there to drone ;
The sky, unbrushed of any wing,
Hung above me like a stone,
And scarce my feet obeyed my will
As heavily I walked alone.

Then, like a tender memory,
Crept up from off the lifeless ground
The low, melodious lovely sound
Of water lapsing secretly.
A little sunken stream I found,
And all the way was sweet to me.

O ancient music earliest heard
Ere tune was born or any bird,
When first above the chaos wild
The brooding spirit breathed and stirred ;
O first-born music, undefiled,
Clear as the laughter of a child,
Fresh as God's latest word !

RICHARD HUGHES

POETS, PAINTERS, PUDDINGS

POETS, painters, puddings; these three
Make up the World as it ought to be.

Poets make faces
And sudden grimaces :
They twit you, and spit you
On words : then admit you
To heaven or hell
By the tales they tell.

Painters are gay
As young rabbits in May ;
They buy jolly mugs,
Bowls, pictures, and jugs :
The things round their necks
Are lively with checks,
(For they like something red
As a frame for the head) :
Or they'll curse you with oaths
That tear holes in your clothes.
(With nothing to mend them
You'd best not offend them.)

Puddings should be
Full of currants, for me :
Boiled in a pail,
Tied in the tail
Of an old bleached shirt ;

So hot that they hurt,
So huge that they laſt
From the dim, diſtant paſt,
Until the crack o' doom
Lift the roof off the room.

Poets, painters, and puddings ; these three
Crown the day as it crowned should be.

HELIODORA

HE and I sought together,
over the spattered table,
rhymes and flowers,
gifts for a name.

He said, among others,
I will bring
(and the phrase was just and good,
but not as good as mine)
'the narcissus that loves the rain.'

We strove for a name
while light of the lamp burnt thin
and the outer dawn came in,
a ghost, the last at the feast
or the first,
to sit within
with the two that remained
to quibble in flowers and verse
over a girl's name.

He said, 'the rain loving,'
I said, 'the narcissus, drunk,
drunk with the rain.'
Yet I had lost
for he said,
'the rose, the lover's gift,
is loved of love,'

he said it,
'loved of love' ;
I waited, even as he spoke,
to see the room filled with a light,
as when in winter
the embers catch in a wind
when a room is dank :
so I thought it would be filled, I thought,
our room with a light
when he said
(and he said it first)
'the rose, the lover's delight,
is loved of love,'
but the light was the same.

Then he caught,
seeing the fire in my eyes,
my fire, my fever, perhaps,
for he leaned
with the purple wine
stained in his sleeve,
and said this :
'Did you ever think
a girl's mouth
caught in a kiss
is a lily that laughs ?'

I had not.
I saw it now
as men must see it forever afterwards ;
no poet could write again,
'the red-lily,

a girl's laugh caught in a kiss' ;
it was his to pour in the vat
from which all poets dip and quaff,
for poets are brothers in this.

So I saw the fire in his eyes,
it was almost my fire
(he was younger) ;
I saw the face so white,
my heart beat,
it was almost my phrase,
I said, 'surprise the muses,
take them by surprise ;
it is late,
rather is it dawn-rise,
those ladies sleep, the nine
our own King's mistresses.'

A name to rhyme,
flowers to bring to a name,
what was one girl faint and shy,
with eyes like the myrtle
(I said : 'her underlids
are rather like myrtle'),
to vie with the nine ?

Let him take the name,
he had the rhymes,
'the rose, loved of love,'
'the lily, a mouth that laughs,'
he had the gift,
' the scented crocus,

the purple hyacinth';
what was one girl to nine?

He said:
'I will make her a wreath;'
he said:
'I will write it thus:
" *I will bring you the lily that laughs,
I will twine
with soft narcissus, the myrtle,
sweet crocus, white violet,
the purple hyacinth, and, last,
the rose, loved of love,
that these may drip on your hair
the less, soft flowers,
may mingle sweet with the sweet
of Heliodora's locks,
myrrh-curled* " '

(He wrote myrrh-curled,
I think, the first).

I said:
'they sleep, the nine.'
When he shouted, swift and passionate:
'*that* for the nine!
Above the mountains
the sun is about to wake,
*and to-day white violets
shine beside white lilies
adrift on the mountain side;
to-day the narcissus opens
that loves the rain.*'

l watched him to the door,
catching his robe
as the wine-bowl crashed to the floor,
spilling a few wet lees
(ah! his purple hyacinth!);
I saw him out of the door,
I thought:
there will never be a poet
in all the centuries after this
who will dare write
after my friend's verse,
'a girl's mouth
is a lily kissed.'

MAXWELL BODENHEIM

FINALITIES

LIKE other men, you fly from adjectives.
The plain terseness that lives in verbs and
nouns
Creates a panorama where you know
That men are not a cloud of romping clowns.
You greet the wideness of eternal curves
Where beauty, death, and silence give their height
To those rare men who do not play with thought.
But this fruit-peddler decorates his freight
And polishes his peaches and his grapes
Insanely. If his mercenary hopes
Were bolder he would be a nimble poet.
Slight in her bridal gown, his mind elopes
With adjectives that find her incomplete.
Your mind is hard, and massively parades
Across the earth with Homer and Villon.
Since each of you with common-sense evades
Monotony, I join you and refuse
To call you dwarf or giant. Let the fools
Who criticize you bind you with these names,
And separate your dead bones with their rules.

GEORGE O'NEIL

WHERE IT IS WINTER

NOW there is frost upon the hill
And no leaf stirring in the wood ;
The little streams are cold and still ;
Never so still has winter stood.
Never so held as in this hollow,
Beneath these hemlocks dark and low,
Brooding this hour that hours must follow
Burdened with snow. . .

Now there is nothing, no confusion,
To shield against the silence here ;
And spirits, barren of illusion,
To whom all agonies are clear,
Rush on the naked heart and cry
Of every poignant shining thing
Where there is little left to die
And no more Spring.

MARY JOHNSTON

VIRGINIANA

S LOW turns the water by the green marshes,
In Virginia.
Overhead the sea fowl
Make silver flashes, cry harsh as peacocks.
Capes and islands stand,
Ocean thunders,
The light houses burn red and gold stars.
In Virginia
Run a hundred rivers.
The dogwood is in blossom,
The pink honeysuckle,
The fringe tree.
My love is the ghostly armed sycamore,
My loves are the yellow pine and the white pine,
My love is the mountain linden.
Mine is the cedar.
Ancient forest,
Hemlock-mantled cliff,
Black cohosh,
Golden-rod, ironweed,
And purple farewell-summer.
Maple red in the autumn,
And plunge of the mountain brook.

The wind bends the wheat ears,
The wind bends the corn,
The wild grape to the vineyard grape
Sends the season's greetings.

Timothy, clover,
Apple, peach!
The blue grass talks to the moss and fern.

Sapphire-shadowed, deep-bosomed, long-limbed,
Mountains lie in the garden of the sky,
Evening is a passion flower, morning is a rose!

Old England sailed to Virginia,
Bold Scotland sailed,
Vine-wreathed France sailed,
And the Rhine sailed,
And Ulster and Cork and Killarney.
Out of Africa—out of Africa!
Guinea Coast, Guinea Coast,
Senegambia, Dahomey.—
Now One,
Now Virginia!

Pocahontas steals through the forest,
Along the Blue Ridge ride the Knights of the Horse-
      shoe,
Young George Washington measures neighbour's
      land from neighbour,
In the firelight Thomas Jefferson plays his violin.
Violin, violin!
Patrick Henry speaks loud in Saint John's church.
Andrew Lewis lifts his flint lock.—
O Fringed Hunting Shirt, where are you going?
George Rogers Clarke takes Kagkaskia and Vin-
      cennes.

They tend tobacco,
And they hoe the corn,
Coloured folk singing,
Singing sweetly of heaven
And the Lord Jesus.
Broad are the tobacco leaves,
Narrow are the corn blades,
Little blue morning glories run through the
        cornfields.

Sumach, sumach !
Blue-berried cedar,
Persimmon and pawpaw,
Chinquepin.
Have you seen the 'possum ?
Have you seen the 'coon ?
Have you heard the whippoorwill ?
Whippoorwill ! Whippoorwill !
Whip—poor—will !

White top waggons
Rolling westward.
Bearded men
Looking westward.
Women, children,
Gazing westward.
Kentucky !
Ohio !
Halt at eve and build the fire.
Dogs,
Long guns,
Household gear.

'Ware the Indian !
White top waggons going westward.

Edgar Allan Poe
Walking in the moonlight,
In the woods of Albemarle,
'Neath the trees of Richmond,
Pondering names of women,
          Annabel—Annie,
          Lenore—Ulalume.

Maury, Maury !
What of Winds and Currents ?
Maury, Maury,
Ocean rover !
But when you come to die,
'Carry me through Goshen Pass
When the rhododendron is in bloom !'

Men in gray,
Men in blue,
Very young men,
Meet by a river.
Overhead are fruit trees.
'Water—water !
We will drink, then fight.'—
'O God, why do we
Fight anyhow ?
It's a good swimming hole
And the cherries are ripe !'
Bronze men on bronze horses,
Down the long avenue,

They ride in the sky,
Bronze men.
Stuart cries to Jackson,
Jackson cries to Lee,
Lee cries to Washington.
Bronze men,
Great soldiers.

The church bells ring,
In Virginia.
Sonorous,
Sweet,
In the sunshine,
In the rain.
Salvation ! It is Sunday.
Salvation ! It is Sunday,
In Virginia.
Locust trees in bloom,
Long grass in the church yard,
June bugs zooning round the roses,
First bell—second bell !
All the ladies are in church.
Now the men will follow,
In Virginia,
In Virginia !

MURIEL STUART

LEDA

Do you remember, Leda ?

WHERE are those who love, to whom Love brings
  Great gladness : such thing have not I.
Love looks and has no mercy, brings
Long doom to others. Such was I.
Heart-breaking hand upon the lute
Touching one note only . . . such were you.
Who shall play now upon that lute
Long last made musical by you ?
Sharp bird-beak in the swelling fruit,
Blind frost upon the eyes of flowers,
Who shall now praise the shrivelled fruit,
Or lift the eyelids of those flowers ?

I dare not watch that hidden pool,
Nor see the wild bird's sudden wing
Lifting the wide, brown, shaken pool.
But round me falls that secret wing,
And in the sharp, perverse, sweet pain
That is half-terror and half-bliss,
My withered hands are curled on pain
That were so wide once after bliss.
And gold is springing in my hair
As my thoughts spring and flower with it,
Though I sit hid in my grey hair,
Without love or the pain of it.
Yet, oh my Swan, if love have wings,

As the gods tell us, you were love
Who took and broke me with those wings.
I, weak, and being far gone in love,
Let blushless things be breathed and done—
Things flowered out now in bitter fruit,
That once done are no more undone
Than last year's frost and last year's fruit.

For what has come of love and me
Who knew the first joy that loving is ?
Where has love led and beckoned me
But to the end where nothing is ?
I have seen my blood beat out again
Red in the hands of all my line,
My sin has swelled and flowered again
Corrupt and fierce through Sparta's line.
Bred through me—bred through delicate hands
And wandering eyes and wanton lips
Sighing after strange flesh as sighed these lips,
Straying after new sin as strayed these hands.
Mother of Helen ! She whose breasts
To new desires unshaped the world,
Above Troy's summits towered these breasts—
Helen who wantoned with the world !
Helen is dead (she had love enough
To laugh at doom and mock at shrine),
And Clytemnestra, quiet enough
To-night beneath Apollo's shrine.
And I am left, the source, the spring
Of all their madness. They are dead
While I still sit here, the old spring
That fouled them flows above the dead.

But I have paid. I have borne enough,
I am very old in love and woe.
For all souls these things are enough—-
Who have known love are the friends of woe.
There are those who love, and who escape,
There are those who love and do not die.
I loved, and there was no escape,
Long since I died and daily die.
And death alone makes hate and love
Friends with each other and with sleep . . .
All's quiet here that once was love,
This that is left belongs to sleep.

CARL SANDBURG

MOON-RIDERS

I

WHAT have I saved out of a morning ?
The earliest of the morning came with moon-
mist
And the travel of a moon-spilt purple :
Bars, horse-shoes, Texas long-horns,
Linked in night silver,
Linked under leaves in moonlit silver,
Linked in rags and patches
Out of the ice-houses of the morning moon.
Yes, this was the earliest—
Before the cowpunchers on the eastern rims
Began riding into the sun,
Riding the roan mustangs of morning,
Roping the mavericks after the latest stars.
What have I saved out of a morning ?
Was there a child face I saw once
Smiling up a stairway of the morning moon ?

II

'It is time for work,' said a man in the morning.
He opened the faces of the clocks, saw their works,
Saw the wheels oiled and fitted, running smooth.
'It is time to begin a day's work,' he said again,
Watching a bullfinch hop on the rain-worn boards
Of a beaten fence counting its bitter winters.

The clinging feet of the bullfinch and the flash
Of its flying feathers as it flipped away
Took his eyes away from the clocks—his flying eyes.
He walked over, stood in front of the clocks again,
And said, 'I'm sorry ; I apologize forty ways.'

III

The morning paper lay bundled,
Like a spear in a museum,
Across the broken sleeping-room
Of a moon-sheet spider.
The spinning work of the morning spider's feet
Left off where the morning paper's pages lay
In the shine of the web in the summer-dew grass.
The man opened the morning paper: saw the first
        page,
The back page, the inside pages, the editorials ;
Saw the world go by, eating, stealing, fighting ;
Saw the headlines, date-lines, funnies, ads,
The marching movies of the workmen going to
        work, the workmen striking,
The workmen asking jobs—five million pairs of eyes
        look for a boss and say, 'Take *me*';
People eating with too much to eat, people eating
        with nothing in sight to eat to-morrow, eating
        as though eating belongs where people belong.

'Hustle, you hustlers, while the hustling's good,'
Said the man, turning the morning paper's pages,
Turning among headlines, date-lines, funnies, ads.
'Hustlers carrying the banner,' said the man,

Dropping the paper and beginning to hunt the city ;
Hunting the alleys, boulevards, back-door by-ways ;
Hunting till he found a blind horse dying alone,
Telling the horse, 'Two legs or four legs—it's all the
    same with a work plug.'

A hayfield mist of evening saw him
Watching the moon-riders lose the moon
For new shooting-stars. He asked,
'Christ, what have I saved out of a morning ?'
He called up a stairway of the morning moon,
And he remembered a child face smiling up that same
    stairway.

RUTH HARWOOD

THE SHOE FACTORY

Song of the Knot-Tyer

THEY told me
When I came
That this would be drudgery,
Always the same
Things over and over,
Day after day—
The same swift movement
In the same small way.

Pick up,
Place,
Push,
And it's tied.
Take off,
Cut,
And put
It aside.

Over and over,
In rhythmical beat—
Some say it is drudgery,
But to me it is sweet.

Pick up,
Place,
Push,
And it's tied.

Outdoors
   The sky
      Is so blue
         And so wide !

It's a joyous song
   Going steadily on,
Marching in measures
   Till the day is gone.

Pick up,
   Place,
      Push,
         And it's tied.
Soon end
   Of day
      Will bring him
         To my side.

Oh, I love the measures
   Singing so fast,
Speeding happy hours
   Till he comes at last !

GWENDOLEN HASTE

MONTANA WIVES

Horizons

I HAD to laugh,
For when she said it we were sitting by the door,
And straight down was the Fork
Twisting and turning and gleaming in the sun.
And then your eyes carried across to the purple
    bench beyond the river
With the Beartooth Mountains fairly screaming with
    light and blue and snow,
And fold and turn of rimrock and prairie as far as
    your eye could go.
And she says : 'Dear Laura, sometimes I feel so sorry
    for you,
Shut away from everything—eating out your heart
    with loneliness.
When I think of my own full life I wish that you
    could share it.
Just pray for happier days to come, and bear it.'

She goes back to Billings to her white stucco house,
And looks through net curtains at another white
    stucco house,
And a brick house,
And a yellow frame house,
And six trimmed poplar trees,
And little squares of shaved grass.

Oh dear, she stared at me like I was daft.
I couldn't help it ! I just laughed and laughed.

LEONORA SPEYER

PROTEST IN PASSING

THIS house of flesh was never loved of me !
This frail white arrogance of sounding towers,
How it has held me through the ordained hours
That I must pass to whiter dignity.
When sleep came beckoning, how I leapt, for then
I knew the low, half-flights of hampered wing,
But now there comes a surer Beckoning,
I go, nor shall endure these rooms again.

I have been held too long by closed-in walls,
By masonry of muscle, blood and bone,
This quaking house of flesh that was my own—
High roof-tree of the heart, see, how it falls !
I go . . . but pause upon the threshold's rust
To shake from off my feet my own dead dust.

MARTIN ARMSTRONG

POETRY AND THE SUBCONSCIOUS

DARK is the mind's deep dwelling,
   Roofed and walled and floored
With ancient rock. There water, slowly welling
   Or slowly dripped, is stored
In a dim, deep, dreaming pool
Unvexed by rain or sunlight or the cool
Wings of the winds, untroubled by joy or grieving,
Or the bitterness or the ecstasy of living.

Till the white young bathers come, warily treading,
   Lovely, desired, with rosy flesh
Like the apple-bloom on the grey bough spreading
   In April, and their feet refresh
Like April the grey desert place.

But when with a sudden freakish grace
They break the pool's long sleep in an airy flight
   Of diving, the dim pool takes light,
Blooms to soft fire in a thousand curves unfurled
That shed a glimmering beauty on roof and walls,
   And rouse in these stern halls
Laughing music of water, and the death
   Of that dark underworld
Thrills harplike with new ecstasy and the breath
   Of a thousand buds uncurled.

PASCAL D'ANGELO

MIDDAY

THE road is like a little child running ahead of me
    and then hiding behind a curve—
Perhaps to surprise me when I reach there.

The sun has built a nest of light under the eaves of
    noon ;
A lark drops down from the cloudless sky
Like a singing arrow, wet with blue, sped from the
    bow of space.

But my eyes pierce the soft azure, far, far beyond,
To where roam eternal lovers
Along the broad blue ways
Of silence.

PASCAL D'ANGELO

LIGHT

EVERY morning, while hurrying along River
    Road to work,
I pass the old miser Stemowski's hut,
Beside which pants a white perfumed cloud of
    acacias.
And the poignant spring pierces me.

My eyes are suddenly glad, like cloud-shadows when
    they meet the sheltering gloom
After having been long stranded in a sea of glassy
    light.

Then I rush to the yard.
But on the job my mind still wanders along the steps
    of dreams in search of beauty.
O how I bleed in anguish ! I suffer.
Amid my happy, laughing but senseless toilers !
Perhaps it is the price of a forbidden dream sunken
    in the purple sea of an obscure future.

ANN HAMILTON

PAUSE

QUICK, for the tide is sifting down the shore,
  Water and wind and vapoury lift of spray—
Flowing of light with darkness through the door,
Sun or moon at the window, night and day—
Quick, while the shadow tangles in and out
Over this threshold that the rain has worn,
Whisper or threaten, trust or pray or doubt,
Still will some men be dead, and some be born ;
Give me your eyes unmasked, and wonder well
How we are brief antagonists of Fate.
Friendship ? But what is friendship ? Can you tell ?
Look at the hinges rusting on the gate ;
Quick then, this breath, while we believe we know—
Kiss through your laughter, kiss again—and go.

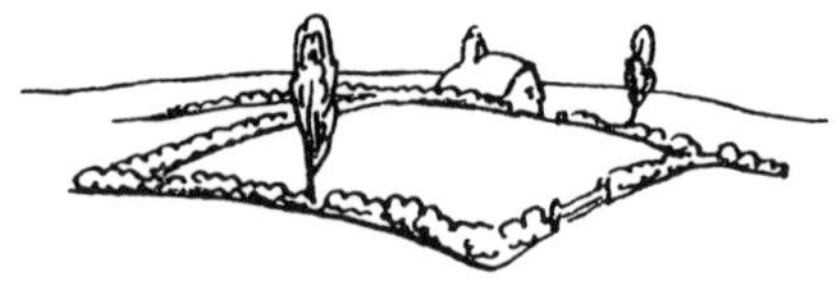

A. E. COPPARD

THE YOUNG MAN UNDER THE WALNUT-TREE

OBSERVE the rotund galleries of this walnut-
    tree,
Its shales of dull stiff wax
Ushering a pool of air, a pool and a green pavilion,
Wherein, sweet tyrant sun, the majesty of shade
Dips a forefinger gilded with your bloom
To paint her modest brows.

Behold the wimpling rye,
The ewes, the poppies steeped in flagrant sun,
Silent, silent, silent ; but the lark
Flying as it sings, singing only as it flies,
Spices with diamond noise the gleaming air.
O golden world, that in your glorious dust
Treasures the trick of Being,
How we, all credulous, obey you !
We are but the habits of the earth,
Its passion for similitude,
For forms and forms again and forms.
This fond bereavement from oblivion,
This thrusting of pale buds from out the branching
    darkness,
Was once with languor, with besieging sleep,
Lapped like a dream within a dream
Till life, life in a splendid pause,
Began its crepitation,
Broke into form, engendering from the dust
Walnuts and things like me,

This clutching honeysuckle drunken-fumed,
The blind newt moving,
And martins marvellous in the sky.

O wild sweet dust,
Dreaming the unsleeping dream
Of flagrant poppy, honeysuckle, breeze,
Bird in the rye, earth, life, oblivion,
From you we follow and flow,
To you we falter and fall ;
You who are full of love,
Love that is born of wonder and dies on the empty
        air.

But love shall have days of honour
Ere the defeat of love,
And fine nights to dream in
Her deep bed of rest.

ALICE MEYNELL

HERE are my thoughts, alive within this fold,
My simple sheep. Their shepherd, I grow wise
As dearly, gravely, deeply I behold
    Their different eyes.

Oh distant pastures in their blood ! Oh streams
From watersheds that fed them for this prison !
Lights from aloft, midsummer suns in dreams,
    Set and arisen.

They wander out, but all return anew,
The small ones, to this heart to which they clung ;
' And those that are with young,' the fruitful few
    That are with young.

BEN RAY REDMAN

SEAWARD

PASSING along the shore,
With undivergent steps, and eyes incurious,
How many fail
To glimpse the pagan sail
Of Beauty, riding over distant wave.

A sail that tempts the swimmer
To essay the sea ;
Woven of gold and crimson rapturously ;
Shot through with magic threads,
Ravished from dreams,
It seems
A flame of deathless ecstasy
That rides afar elusively.

But when we do attempt the deep,
'Tis with sure knowledge we must fail ;
Though in our last defeat we keep
At least the image of the sail,
Golden and crimson that we fought to reach
And, when at last we're flung back on the beach,
Or when, half way, we meet deep death,
Still thrusting forward with our parting breath ;
Facing our failure with a brave surprise
We die with Beauty mirrored in our eyes.

LILL' ANGELS

MAMMY rocks the baby
  In the wallflower-coloured gloom ;
All the floor rocks with her,
  And the slumber of the room.
Like the broad, unceasing trade-wind,
  Like the rivers underground,
Rolls the universal rhythm
  And the rich, primeval sound :
    All de lill' angels,
    All de baby's angels,
      Swingin' on de tree ;
    Forty-one lill' angel',
    Fifty-two lill' angel',
    Sixty-fo' lill' angel',
      Sebbenty-t'ree. . . .

On the glory of the sundown,
  Of the wallflower-coloured skies
I can see her vast Assumption
  In a cloud of cherubs' eyes.
With their gold-persimmon haloes
  Where the ripest sunlight falls,
And the cherub-tree's espaliered
  On the winking crystal walls.
    Little yaller angels,
    Piccaninny angels,
      Chuckle in the tree.
    Forty-one lill' angel',
    Fifty-two lill' angel',
    Sixty-fo' lill' angel',
      Se . . . ebbenty-t'ree. . . .

CHARLES WHARTON STORK

GREEN FIRE

YOU are April,
Green fire,
A flame that flickers, glitters,
But never glows.

You are a ripple on the sea of Beauty
That clasps and cradles the light
On the bent mirror of its emerald bosom
With an eager gesture of dancing,
Then tosses it lightly away
Like a silver veil.

And you are the upward lilt
Of a delicious voice,
A flutter of lark-sweet laughter
As light as floating thistle-down.

Do I wish, I wonder,
That you should be May,
Should send out a bud of golden passion,
Should rise and break in a billow of foaming ecstasy?
Or would I have your music sound more deep
As from the wounded breast of lyric pain?

I cannot tell,
I cannot see past you now,
Because I must always look at you as you are,
My April,
My flame that flickers, gleams, but never glows.

EDWARD SHANKS

WOMAN'S SONG

NO more upon my bosom rest thee,
Too often have my hands caressed thee,
    My lips thou knowest well, too well ;
Lean to my heart no more thine ear
My spirit's living truth to hear
    —It has no more to tell.

In what dark night, in what strange night,
Burnt to the butt the candle's light
    That lit our room so long ?
I do not know. I thought I knew
How love could be both sweet and true ;
    I also thought it strong.

Where has the flame departed ? Where,
Amid the empty waste of air,
    Is that which dwelt with us ?
Was it a fancy ? Did we make
Only a show for dead love's sake,
    It being so piteous ?

No more against my bosom press thee,
Seek no more that my hands caress thee,
    Leave the sad lips thou hast known so well ;
If to my heart thou lean thine ear,
There grieving thou shalt only hear
    Vain murmuring of an empty shell.

MARX G. SABEL

RECORDITION

I HAVE hailed you.
Out of centuries, out of aeons,
During this fractional part of an infinitesimal clock-
    tick of tune,
I have seen you,
And hailed you.

I have yearned toward you,
Burning.
I have looked into your eyes
During this fractional part of an infinitesimal clock-
    tick of time.

Quicker than the shadow of a monoplane
Passing over the shadow of a humming bird
Shall we two pass,
And be to all men's memory
Inconceivably remote.

Yet it is recorded
That out of all time,
During this fractional part of an infinitesimal clock-
    tick of time,
I have seen you and hailed you.
It is recorded.

THOMAS HARDY

WHERE once we danced, where once we sang,
      Gentlemen,
The floors are sunken, cobwebs hang,
And cracks creep ; worms have fed upon
The doors. Yea, sprightlier times were then
Than now, with harps and tabrets gone,
      Gentlemen !

Where once we rowed, where once we sailed,
      Gentlemen,
And damsels took the tiller, veiled
Against too strong a stare (God wot
Their fancy, then or anywhen !)
Upon that shore we are clean forgot,
      Gentlemen !

We have lost somewhat, afar and near,
      Gentlemen,
The thinning of our ranks each year
Affords a hint we are nigh undone,
That we shall not be ever again
The marked of many, loved of one,
      Gentlemen.

In dance the polka hit our wish,
      Gentlemen,
The paced quadrille, the spry schottische,
'Sir Roger.'—And in opera spheres
The 'Girl' (the famed 'Bohemian '),
And 'Trovatore,' held the ears,
      Gentlemen.

This season's paintings do not please,
          Gentlemen,
Like Etty, Mulready, Maclise ;
Throbbing romance has waned and wanned ;
No wizard wields the witching pen
Of Bulwer, Scott, Dumas, and Sand,
          Gentlemen.

The bower we shrined to Tennyson,
          Gentlemen,
Is roof-wrecked ; damps there drip upon
Sagged seats, the creeper-nails are rust,
The spider is sole denizen ;
Even she who read those rhymes is dust,
          Gentlemen !

We who met sunrise sanguine-souled,
          Gentlemen,
Are wearing weary. We are old ;
These younger press ; we feel our rout
Is imminent to Aïdes' den,—
That evening's shades are stretching out,
          Gentlemen !

And yet, though ours be failing frames,
          Gentlemen,
So were some others' history names,
Who trode their track light-limbed and fast
As these youth, and not alien
From enterprise, to their long last,
          Gentlemen.

Sophocles, Plato, Socrates,
        Gentlemen,
Pythagoras, Thucydides,
Herodotus, and Homer,—yea,
Clement, Augustin, Origen,
Burnt brightlier towards their setting-day,
        Gentlemen.

And ye, red-lipped and smooth-browed ; list,
        Gentlemen ;
Much is there waits you we have missed ;
Much lore we leave you worth the knowing,
Much, much has lain outside our ken :
Nay, rush not : time serves ; we are going,
        Gentlemen.

ALFRED KREYMBORG

BLOOM

WHEN flowers thrust their heads above the
        ground
in showers pale as raindrops, and as round,
who would suspect that such, before they're gone,
could hold the sun ?

So fine a pressure from above can bring
so frail a thing to push its way aloft ?—
through clay, a woman might consider cloth
for constant stitching ?

Right straight down and right straight up again,
through holes so close, no manly eye can see
the bloom come out of needles—or can she
be using rain ?

And now that she still labours in the gloom,
her room just lighted by the sun turned moon—
need any man be told what flowers are,
that hold a star ?

DOROTHY DOW

TO ATALANTA

YOU, Atalanta, were so fleet.
Lend the magic of your feet,
Lend your rushing sandals slim
That I may outdistance him.

I would race with him, and show
How much faster I can go.

Then, when he, all wearily
Stops to rest beneath a tree,
Whisper to him that I will
Wait . . . beyond the farthest hill.

DOROTHY ROBERTS

TOWN GARDEN

HOW wondrously the next-door man has grown
A garden for himself, where bricks were thrown
And bottles and old hoops ! I watched him dig
When winter's rain hung on each poplar twig,
And one wise robin followed him all day
To catch the worms his big spade threw away.

How joyfully I saw the streak of gold,
Pale as the line spring clouds at sundown hold,
That grew and brightened on each barren bed,
As the light grew and the first sunbeams spread,
Till gold and purple in straight ribbons ran,
And, for his planting, crocuses began.

He made an archway for the rambler rose,
And cut the pebble pathway where he goes
All day among his plants, knowing them all.
He hears from his one tree a blackbird's call,
For June is come, and these first wonder flowers
Have charmed a singer from green country bowers.

So day by day I watch the summer grow
Down in the new-made garden. Now I know
How lad's love at sundown scents the slow night,
How little elder shrubs have golden light,
How violas stay long, how poppies die,
And scatter with the first wind's passing by.

And here, I'm told, at the late summer's turn,
In dark red smouldering fire, dahlias will burn,
And tall chrysanthemums, awaiting flower,
Will drink the rain for beauty, shower on shower;
And when the first leaves fall and creep below,
Great sunflower eyes will watch the summer go.

CARLYLE McINTYRE

THE SCISSOR-GRINDER

THE scissor-man tramped into town. Ding-a-
dong ! ding-a-dong !
He set his little grindstone down, and to its music
  hummed a song.

Old Grandma Dumpkins' scissor-shears, he edged
  their blades so finely,
That she cut off her children's ears and made them
  sing divinely.

And Gaffer Smither's pruning-hook he whetted to
  such keenness
That Gaffer trimmed the town, and took the shade
  for meanness.

But furthermore, the butcher's knife he rounded off
  so dully,
That cattle now enjoy their life and fill the milkpails
  fully.

Then—ding-a-dong ! ding-a-dong ! I saw his red
  hat top the hill ;
But all night long I heard his song played by his
  brother watermill.

JOSEPH AUSLANDER

IS THIS THE LARK!

IS this the lark
Lord Shakespeare heard
Out of the dark
Of dawn ! Is this the bird
That stirred
Lord Shakespeare's heart !

Is this the bird whose wing,
Whose rapturous antheming,
Rose up, soared radiant, became
Sharp flame
To Shelley listening,
And made him sing,
Throbbing alone, aloof, feveredly apart,
His profuse strains of unpremeditated art !

To think that I should hear him now
Telling that single fiery rift of heaven a wild lark
    comes ! . . .
The fresh cool scent of earth yearns at the plough ;
In short keen rapid flurries the woodpecker
    drums . . .
To think that I should hear that mad thing sliding
Along a smoking opal ladder !
Hear that inevitable deluge of music riding
Into the sun, richer now—fainter now—madder !
To think that I should hear and know
The song that Shelley heard, and Shakespeare, long
    ago !

SANCTUARY

GOD has builded a House with a low lintel,
And in it He has put all manner of things ;
Follow the clue through the mazes that lead to His door,
Look in ! Look in ! See what is there for our finding.
Peace is there like a pearl, and rest and the end of
    seeking ;
Light is there and refreshment. But there shall be more;
There we shall find for our use wide, beautiful wings,
Ecstasy, solitude, space ; and for those who have
    been too lonely,
The love of friends, the warmth of a homely fire.

Oh, never grieve again for the piteous ending
Of loveliness that could not be made to laſt ;
There all bright passing beauty is held forever
Free from the sense of tears—to be loved without
    regret.
There shall we find at their source music and love
    and laughter,
Colour and subtle fragrance and soft incredible tex-
    tures.
Be sure we shall find what our weary hearts desire ;
If we are tired of light, there shall be velvet darkness
Falling over long fields, with ſtars, and a low voice
    calling,
Calling at laſt the word we thought would never be
    spoken.
But we, being hard and foolish and proud and mortal,
Are slow to bend and enter that humble portal.

RUTH MANNING-SANDERS

THE DRAKE

THE green-tailed drake looks out of the coop,
   Lifting his head, bobbing his head—
The green-tailed drake is two years old,
   It's time he were fattened and dead.
Out through the coop looks the green-tailed drake,
   And his eyes are like jewels that shine in the wake
Of the long, rhythmic line of the ducks,
     Waddling away,
     Paddling away,
     With a loop round the fence and a loop beyond,
     Waddling away to the pond.

The green-tailed drake cries 'Wait, wait, wait!'
   Opening his beak, shutting his beak,
But the ducks are earnestly talking of snails,
   And his voice comes muffled and weak.
'Wait, wait, wait!' cries the green-tailed drake,
   And his eyes are like fires that burn in the wake
Of the cool, scattering splash of the ducks,
     Swimming away,
     Away and away,
     Swimming away on the pond.

DAVID MORTON

THESE FIELDS AT EVENING

THESE wear their evening light as women wear
Their pale proud beauty for some lover's sake,
Too quiet-hearted evermore to care
For moving worlds and musics that they make ;
And they are hushed as lonely women are—
So lost in dreams they have no thought to mark
How the wide heavens blossom, star by star,
And the slow dusk is deepening to the dark.

The moon comes like a lover from the hill,
Leaning across the twilight and the trees ;
And finds them grave and beautiful and still,
And wearing always, on such nights as these,
A glimmer less than any ghost of light,
As women wear their beauty through the night.

EDMUND BLUNDEN

COUNTRY SALE

UNDER the thin green sky, the twilight day,
The old home lies in public sad array,
Its time being come, the lots ranged out in rows,
And to each lot a ghost. The gathering grows
With every minute, neckcloths and gold pins ;
Poverty's purples ; red necks, horny skins,
Odd peering eyes, thin lips and hooking chins.
Then for the skirmish, and the thrusting groups
Bidding for tubs and wire and chicken coops,
While yet the women hang apart and eye
Old friends and foes and reckon what they'll buy.
The noisy field scarce knows itself, and none
Takes notice of the old man's wavering moan
Who hobbles with his hand still brushing tears
And cries how this belonged here sixty years,
And picks his brother's picture from the mass
Of frames ; and still from heap to heap folks pass.

The strife of tongues even tries the auctioneer,
Who, by the dealer smirking to his leer,
A jumped-up jerky cockerel on his box,
Runs all his rigs, cracks all his jokes and mocks :
'Madam, now never weary of well-doing,'
The heavy faces gleam to hear him crowing.
And swift the old home's fading. Here he bawls
The white four-poster, with its proud recalls,
But folks on such old-fashioned lumber frown ;
'Passing away at a florin,' grins the clown.

Here Baskett's Prayer Book with his black and red
Finds no more smile of welcome than the bed,
Though policeman turn the page with wisdom's
        looks—
The hen-wives see no use in such old books.
Here painted trees, and well-feigned towers arise,
And ships before the wind that sixpence buys.

All's sold ; then hasty vanmen pile and rope
Their loads, and ponies stumble up the slope.
And all are gone, the trampled paddock's bare ;
The children round the buildings run and blare,
Thinking what times these are ! not knowing how
The heavy-handed fate has brought them low,
Till quartern loaf be gone too soon to-day,
Nor any for to-morrow.—Long then play,
And make the lofts re-echo through the eve,
And sweeten so the bitter taking-leave.

So runs the world away. Years hence shall find
The mother weeping to her lonely mind
In some new place, thin set with makeshift gear,
For the home she had before the fatal year ;
And still to this same anguish she'll recur,
Reckoning up her fine old furniture,
The tall clock with his church-bell time of day,
The mirror where so deep the image lay,
The china with its rivets numbered all,
Seeming to have them in her hands—poor soul,
Trembling and crying how these, loved so long,
So beautiful, all went for an old song.

RICHARD ALDINGTON

A SOPHISTRY OF DURATION

TELL me not beauty dies like dew
    The envious sun draws trembling up,
Nor liken hers to that brief hue
    Flushes the rose's tender cup—
For things like her so lovely are,
They should outlive the braveſt ſtar.

If all my senses ſtill conspire,
    Ere their meridian be paſt,
To set the blossoms of desire,
    The worm shall not exult at laſt :
Her children and my words I truſt
Shall speak her grace when we are duſt.

HORTENSE FLEXNER

POETS

EARTH, you have had great lovers in your hour,
And little lovers, fearful and struck dumb ;
Those who have seen you whole, as from a tower,
And others kneeling where the grass blades come.
Age after spinning age and day by day,
They toss the dawn between them, as a ball,
Ride Beauty plunging to the whip of May,
And string the stars to light their carnival.
They will not heed the shouting, singing flood
Of lovers gone before them. Echoed cries,
Too like their own may sound, but their wild blood
Is out of hand at seas and moving skies ;
The last to come will make his little tune,
And think it new—about the weary moon !

LOUIS GOLDING

DOOM-DEVOTED

I WEEP a sight which was not seen,
  A deed which was not done at all,
The murder of an unborn queen,
   The sack of an unbuilded hall.

Never a queen of Art or Song
   This doom-devoted star hath borne
Whom the protagonists of Wrong
   Did not tread down with hooves of scorn.

Stern watch those iron traitors keep
   Who crucified the Singing Child.
The Unborn Christs we poets weep,
   The strangled songs, the dreams defiled.

W. FORCE STEAD

LOVE IN OLD AGE

SO old they were, and every child from home,
The neighbours feared for them, and used to
  come
With proffered help at housework, or to lift
Their garden roots. But they would still make shift,
And manage by themselves. For sixty years
They had been man and wife, and felt no fears
Together in their cottage.—Aye, so old,
They hardly knew when they were ill or cold,
Nor saw how blurred grew each familiar thing,
Nor how they groped thro’ life’s late glimmering.

When they, together, such long years had passed,
Gently he ceased to breathe : they part at last.
The village wives sob thro’ the burial prayer :
Stone-like she stands with a strange vacant stare.

‘Numbed in her mind, her body all but dead,
Little she knows, and little feels,’ I said.

But when the verger swung his spade, amid
The cold earth rattling on the coffin-lid,
Nearer she crept, leaned over the grave-side,
And dropt a simple sprig of green, and cried.

IANTHE JERROLD

ON EPSOM DOWN

GIVE me a penny, kind lady !
Pretty lady, ye've got a lucky smile !
There's a rich man comin', an' a fine big house,
For you, in a little while.
Ah, me mother's broke her arm, kind lady,
So she can't go bikkenin to town.
An' me father's lost a horse, lady. Look in yer purse,
An' throw me a halfpenny down.

You can keep your house, little gipsy,
And your fine rich man also.
I'll have a little cottage where woods meet downs
With a dear, poor lad I know.
And as for your tale, little gipsy,
I know very well it's lies,
But I'll give you a penny for your rough brown hair,
And a penny for your bright brown eyes !

EVELYN UNDERHILL

WHITSUN-EVE

COME with birds' voices when the light grows
    dim,
  Yet lovelier in departure and more dear ;
While the warm flush hangs still at heaven's rim
  And the one star shines clear.

Though the swift night haste to awaiting day
  Stay thou and stir not, brooding on the deep ;
Thy secret lore, thy living word let say
  Within the senses' sleep

Softer than dew. But when the morning wind
  Blows down the world, O Spirit, show thy power !
Quicken the dreams within the languid mind,
  And bring thy seed to flower.

ISOBEL HUME

WHITENESS

THE little betrothed has washed her linen—
  And hung it out to dry,
It puffs and blows into mists and cloudlets
  Under the April sky.

Her arms are white as the white pear-blossom—
  Her throat is as white as may ;
And her heart, like a song on a sunny morning,
  New-born and sweet as they.

She will walk in white to church on Sunday
  Through orchards where birds sing :
And the bridegroom, taking her home at evening—
  Will think he weds the Spring.

JOHN FREEMAN

WILLOW droops now her breast upon the breast
Of waveless water,
Leaning her cheek against that hueless cheek ;
And her leaves speak
Tender as silence when the least wind trembles
And sinks at rest.

Floats on the stream the rippled argent round
Of the full moon,
Following with slower mood the faltering tide.
Willow's branches slide
Deeper to draw the moon close to her breast,
In silver slumber.

But as a murdered face in agitation
Of windy flaw,
The argent moon wrinkles in angry pain :
Eyes stare in dream of pain.
Wind on the willow's bosom falls and moans,
Hides in a floating cloud the moon's torn face.

PADRAIC COLUM

THE POOR GIRL'S MEDITATION

(*From the Irish*)

I AM sitting here,
Since the moon rose in the night ;
Kindling a fire,
And striving to keep it alight ;
The folks of the house are lying
In slumber deep ;
The cocks will be crowing soon ;
The whole of the land is asleep.

May I never leave this world
Until my ill-luck is gone ;
Till I have cows and sheep,
And the lad that I love for my own ;
I would not think it long,
The night I would lie at his breast,
And the daughters of spite, after that,
Might say the thing they liked best.

Love covers up hate,
If a girl have beauty at all :
On a bed that was narrow and high,
A three-month I lay by the wall :
When I remembered the lad
That I left at the brow of the hill,
I wept from dark until dark,
And my cheeks have the tear-tracks still !

And, O young lad that I love,
I am no mark for your scorn :
All you can say of me
Is undowered I was born :
And if I've no fortune in hand,
Nor cattle or sheep of my own,
This I can say, O lad,
I am fitted to lie my lone !

HILDA CONKLING

SONG NETS

SONG nets,
I weave you with all my love.
You glitter like pearls and rubies,
In you I catch songs like butterflies.
You go past my reaching hand
With a thin gauzy floating.
And the songs are caught
Before they fade away.
Last night
My hand caught a song
Of pines and quiet rivers :
I shall keep it forever.

SNOW MORNING

Morning is a picture again,
With snow-puffed branches
Out of the wind ;
With the sky caught like a blue feather
In the butternut tree.
I cannot see the world behind the snow ;
But when I look into my mind,
There, with all its people and colours,
The world sits smiling
Quite warm and cosy.

Lilies of the valley,
Bell-shaped moments clustered,
Doves of time—little white doves
Through the dusky sunset-coloured air
Set free,
I stroke your wings,
I stroke your folded wings.

LITTLE GREEN BERMUDA POEM

Green water of waves
On the Bermuda beaches,
White coral roads running away,
Pink shells waiting for me to come,
I shall come some day.
How would it sound to be there alone
And hear the Atlantic Ocean
Crash on bright rocks ?

This island is a great rainbow
That lasts forever ;
People go and come
And the waves forget them.
I see the island turn and turn—
A soap-bubble with rainbows drifting down,
A rainbow ball turning . . .
Always light, always glitter looking through.

My poem that began with a green wave
Has broken into colours.

WHEN MOONLIGHT FALLS

When moonlight falls on the water,
It is like fingers touching the chords of a harp
On a misty day.
When moonlight strikes the water
I cannot get it into my poem—
I only hear the tinkle of ripplings of light.
When I see the water's fingers and the moon's rays
Intertwined,
I think of all the words I love to hear
And try to find words white enough
For such shining.

ELSA

My sister stood on a hilltop
Looking toward the sea.
The wind was in her bronze-colored hair :
She was an image
On a broken wave . . .
Foam was at her feet.
So for a moment she wavered
And was lovely :
And I remember her.

CLOUDY-PANSY

Wandering down a dusty road,
I met a gypsy.
She might have dropped out of the trees.
She had a green kerchief
And a blue velvet skirt,

A lavender cape
And a gold locket :
Green shoes on the feet
That trod the powdery road
To the marble-floored Vermont river
Thinking as it goes along . . .

FIELD-MOUSE

Little brown field-mouse
Hiding when the plough goes by,
Timid creature that you are,
Wild thing,
Were you once in the forest ?—
Did you move to the fields ?
In your brown cloak
You gather grain
For your secret meals ;
You will build a house of earth
The way you remember.
From a baby up to your full-grown feeling
You have run about the field,
As other field-mice will run about
When another century has come
Like a cloud.

'I WONDERED AND WONDERED'

I wondered and wondered . . .
I saw a comrade of mine ;
It was a wave smooth and blue
That tossed . . . fell away.
I wondered and wondered . . .

I saw a mountain white with old age :
I could not remember
How I came there.
I wondered and wondered . . .
Under a motherly sky
That knew my name and kind,
That rested my tired thoughts,
That said, 'I have a rainbow for you, Hilda,
And a young moon, hidden.'

J. R. ACKERLEY

ON A PHOTOGRAPH OF MYSELF AS A BOY

HOW young you look! It was not long ago,
   And yet you seem a child, as fresh and fair
As if the gentle spring itself did flow
   Between your lips, and traceries of care
Could never fret your brow. I did not know
   So beautiful you were.

My younger self, what were you musing on
   So gladly in that calm, sequestered place?
Your young beliefs are now forever gone,
   And gone the peace that lighted then your face.
What was the dream for love of which you shone
   With such enchanted grace?

What was the love that stirred within your breast,
   And stole in secret wonder from your eyes,
And moved your lips, and all your limbs caressed,
   And sent its first faint tremor to your thighs,
Like that low vernal music of unrest
   To which the Earth replies?

Let me go back ! Let me go back to you !
   And we will learn some pleasant games to play,
And choose some other fancy to pursue . . .
   O why did you not put your dream away,
Unhappy boy, when it was faint and new,
   And held you not in sway?

You cannot leave it now ; the dream you wrought
  Its spell upon your childish heart has laid,
And you are held enslavèd to your thought,
  And from your eyes its shadow will not fade ;
Forever in that instant are you caught,
  And by that dream betrayed.

VIRGINIA LYNE TUNSTALL

THE OLD SPINNER

ALL around me
  Is the hot room,
And the dust stirred
  By the loud loom.

Yet I am back
  By my own sea,
And a wind comes
  And touches me,

Where the gulls rise
  From the white sand—
Ah, the wind of the loom
  And the tears on my hand !

THESE ARE BUT WORDS . . .

I HAVE a thousand pictures of the sea—
Snatches of song and things that travellers say.
I know its shimmering from green to gray ;
At dawn and sunset it is plain to me.
Like something known and loved for years will be
That sight of it when I shall come some day
Where little waves and great waves war and play,
And little winds and great winds fly out free.

Of love I had no pictures : love would come
Like any casual guest whom I could greet
Serencly, and serenely let depart—
Love, that came like fire and struck me dumb,
That came like wind and swept me from my feet,
That came like lightning shattering my heart.

DOROTHY MARGARET STUART

THE LITTLE TREE

NO taller brethren dwell hard by
　To mock him for his littleness ;
Alone he stands against the sky,
　Sea-dust in every tattered tress.
No Saul among the Sussex trees
　O'ernods him, greaved in mossy bark ;
He buffets with the untempered breeze
　And is lone listener to the lark.

The lark goes climbing up to Heaven,
　Forgetful of the little tree ;
But when she folds her wings at even
　And drops beside him, there is he
With wondering arms outstretched to greet,
　And thorn-flower crownets rosy-pearled,
In silent homage to the sweet
　Singer whose singing wakes the world.

Then when with June his flowers depart
　And with October fly his leaves
He holds stout courage in his heart,
　Nor with the creaking coppice grieves.
When swerving seagulls scream and strive
　O'er the brown furrows driven by men,
His dole of berries keeps alive
　A yellowhammer and a wren.

DAVID MORTON

NEW SORROW

THIS too, in time, will turn an old, sad story,
   Read and re-read and so remembered long ;
This heartbreak, then, will wear a twilight glory,
   And crumbling dust will blur the ugly wrong.
Beauty will be upon it like a spell,
   Blessing the broken turret and the wall,
A grave and healing hush—with none to tell
   What these had been . . . nor how such things
     befall.

I shall come back at some remembering hour,
   Another self among these ruined things,
Noting the late sun on the empty tower,
   The slow dusk and the dead, round moon it brings,
And how all this is beautiful and sad,
   Like some old tale . . . not the sharp grief I had.

FRANCIS BRETT YOUNG

SEASCAPE

OVER that morn hung heaviness, until,
Near sunless noon, we heard the ship's bell
beating
A melancholy staccato on dead metal ;
Saw the bare-footed watch come running aft ;
Felt, far below, the sudden telegraph jangle
Its harsh metallic challenge, thrice repeated :
Stand by. Half-speed ahead. Slow. Stop her ! They
stopped.
The plunging pistons sank like a stopped heart ;
She held, she swayed, a hulk, a hollow carcass
Of blistered iron that the grey-green, waveless,
Unruffled tropic waters slapped languidly.

And, in that pause, a sinister whisper ran :
Burial at sea ! A Portuguese official . . .
Poor fever-broken devil from Mozambique ;
Came on half tight : the doctor calls it heat-stroke.
Why do they travel steerage ? It's the exchange :
So many million *reis* to the pound !
What did he look like ? No one ever saw him :
Took to his bunk, and drank and drank and died.
They're ready ! Silence !
          We clustered to the rail,
Curious and half-ashamed. The well-deck spread
A comfortable gulf of segregation
Between ourselves and death. *Burial at sea . . .*

The master holds a black book at arm's length ;
His droning voice comes for'ard : *This our brother . . .*
We therefore commit his body to the deep
To be turned into corruption. . . .
                 The bo's'n whispers
Hoarsely behind his hand : *Now, all together !*
The hatch-cover is tilted ; a mummy of sail-cloth
Well ballasted with iron shoots clear of the poop ;
Falls, like a diving gannet. The green sea closes
Its burnished skin ; the snaky swell smoothes
      over . . .
While he, the man of the steerage, goes down, down,
Feet foremost, sliding swiftly down the dim water,
Swift to escape
Those plunging shapes with pale, empurpled bellies
That swirl and veer about him. He goes down
Unerringly, as though he knew the way
Through green, through gloom, to absolute watery
     darkness,
Where no weed sways nor curious fin quivers :
To the sad, sunless deeps where, endlessly,
A downward drift of death spreads its wan mantle
In the wave-moulded valleys that shall enfold him
Till the sea give up its dead.

There shall he lie dispersed amid great riches :
Such gold, such arrogance, so many bold hearts !
All the sunken armadas pressed to powder
By weight of incredible seas ! That mingled wrack
No livening sun shall visit till the crust
Of earth be riven, or this rolling planet
Reel on its axis ; till the moon-chained tides,

Unloosed, deliver up that white Atlantis,
Whose naked peaks shall bleach above the slaked
Thirst of Sahara, fringed by weedy tangles
Of Atlas's drown'd cedars, frowning eastward
To where the sands of India lie cold ;
And heap'd Himalaya's a rib of coral
Slowly uplifted, grain on grain . . .

We dream

Too long ! Another jangle of alarum
Stabs at the engines : *Slow*. *Half-speed*. *Full-speed !*
The great bearings rumble ; the screw churns, froth-
   ing
Opaque water to downward-swelling plumes
Milky as woodsmoke. A shoal of flying-fish
Spurts out like animate spray. The warm breeze
   wakens,
And we pass on, forgetting,
Toward the solemn horizon of bronzed cumulus
That bounds our brooding sea, gathering gloom
That, when night falls, will dissipate in flows
Of watery lightning, washing the hot sky,
Cleansing all hearts of heat and restlessness,
Until, with day, another blue be born.

W. H. DAVIES

OUR SUSSEX DOWNS

MY youth is gone—my youth that laughed and yawned
In one sweet breath, and will not come again ;
And crumbs of wonder are my scanty fare,
Snatched from the beauty on a hill or plain.
So, as I look, I wonder if the land
Has *breathed* those shadows in the waters blue !
From all first sounds I half expect to hear,
Not only echoes, but *their* echoes too.
But when I see—the first time in my life—
Our Sussex Downs, so mighty, strong and bare
That many a wood of fifteen hundred trees
Seems but a handful scattered lightly there—
'What a great hour,' think I, 'half-way 'twixt Death
And Youth that laughs and yawns in one short breath.'

WILFRID THORLEY

HANSOM CABBIES

WHEN I was a lad there were hansoms in London,
    With drivers on top of a little back stair
And horses that ran under silver-tipt harness
    Or stood by the kerb-stone awaiting a fare,
    And tossed in the air
        Their nose-bags of corn for the sparrows to
        share.

And sometimes in Spring when the nose-bags were
    leaking,
    And sparrows were loud amid loot of spilt corn,
Old Cabby reached over the slender Park railings
    And stole a rosette of the double red thorn
    His mare to adorn,
        With 'Fares may be few, but we won't be for-
        lorn.'

The spokes they were pointed with red and with
      yellow ;
    The brass was like gold where the reins threaded
      through ;
There was sometimes a crest on the old leather
      blinkers,
    A crown on the horse-cloth of crimson and blue
    That said 'It's for you
        We're waiting, my Lord, and a crown is our
        due.'

Now where are they gone to, the weather-worn
        cabbies
    That drove us alertly through all the dense shoals
That filled the strait Fleet from St. Paul's to St.
        Martin's,
    Or over the bridge where big Benjamin tolls ?
    O ! somewhere their souls
        Still murmur 'Where to, Sir ?' through tiny
        peep-holes.

Elysian fields show them pasturing fillies
    Sure-footed and shapely—just built for a yoke ;
They comb their silk manes and they wheedle and
        drive them
    Down roads without mud where the fogs never
        choke,
    And rain's a rare joke
        To cheerful night-watchmen with cressets of
        coke.

The fares that they find there are born in the purple ;
    Their talk is of Dizzy and Toole and Bend Or ;
Their manners are suave and their tips are all golden ;
    They dwell between Mayfair and Kensington
        Gore ;
    And flunkeys galore
        Poll-powdered, receive them at Paradise door.

G. K. CHESTERTON

' THE MYTH OF ARTHUR '

O LEARNED man who never learned to learn,
  Save to deduce, by timid steps and small,
From towering smoke that fire can never burn
And from tall tales that men were never tall.
Say, have you thought what manner of man it is
Of whom men say 'He could strike giants down'?
Or what strong memories over time's abyss
Bore up the pomp of Camelot and the crown.
But why one banner all the background fills
Beyond the pageants of so many spears,
And by what witchery in the western hills
A throne stands empty for a thousand years.
Who hold, unheeding this immense impact,
Immortal story for a mortal sin ;
Lest human fable touch historic fact,
Chase myths like moths, and fight them with a pin.
Take comfort ; rest—there needs not this ado.
You shall not be a myth, I promise you.

ALAN PORTER

(To Edith Sitwell)

LEARN, all Time's vagrants, where to look ;
   And more, learn what to see—
Hard ground in a pale drudging brook,
   Light in the substance of a tree.

Earth was ashen, mind a mist,
   And mist the only day ;
In every song a satirist,
   Man but a motionable clay.

Almost I had put out these eyes,
   The sun's own fury failed ;
Slayer of childhood, father of lies,
   Reason babbled and prevailed.

From this dark pride and stubborn dearth
   Slowly my self was freed ;
For Clare uncovered infinite worth
   In a cold worm, a common weed.

The minute wealth of nature there
   With a new symbol smiles.
You, Edith, my interpreter,
   Reveal the lost unfabled isles.

Now the dew falls in beads of gold,
   In clear blue stone the rain.
Wind and colour, heat and cold,
   Are flesh, no phantoms of the brain.

I travel through my native woods
   And laugh all day to mark
The squirrel sputter in cross moods,
   Or hear the happy woodlark.

Hard by grow many an Indian flower,
   Cedar and upas :
Heraldic lions, hour by hour,
   Trample down the yellow grass.

Philemon still in some white glade
   And Baucis, knee by knee,
Sit here content as youth and maid,
   Yet hospitable, too, to me.

All Sense, all Fame, all Vision here,
   Inseparable, triune,
Fashion from chaos, firm and clear,
   This only earth, and sun, and moon.

For, truth, he's curst or Antichrist
   Who needs a more or less,
Demands a world anatomised,
   And calls the body nakedness.

What though sight dazzle and words fail ?
   Beauty he knows who can
Hold fast by every traveller's tale,
   The world's one cosmopolitan.

J. C. SQUIRE

TO A ROMAN

I

YOU died two thousand years ago, Catullus,
    Myriads since then have walked the earth you
      knew
All their long lives and faded into nothing,
    And still across that waste men think of you.

You loved your Sirmio, and loved your brother,
    You gave a pitiless woman all your heart ;
You wrote for her, you mourned a sparrow for her,
    Served like a slave : and suffering made your art.

Some fiery songs, a few soft elegies,
    Perfect—you said you used a pumice-stone :
Coarse little squibs, a rosy song for a wedding,
    What else you did, it never will be known.

A proud young man of fashion, whom a woman
    Played with and dropped : nothing remains beside ;
Only we know, about a certain year,
    You went away, out of the sun, and died ;

And all your world died after, all the towers
    Fell, and the temples mouldered, and the games
Left the great circus empty, and the dust
    Buried the Cæsars, senators, and dames.

I see you lying under marble arches,
    Above the bright blue meadow of a bay,
With certain supercilious gross companions
    Talking their filth more cleverly than they.

Amusing them, one of them, seeming with them :
    They are pleased to find Catullus of their kind ;
They sprawl and drink and sneer and jest of wenches,
    Pose to you : but they do not hear your mind.

You share debauch, debauch does not distract you,
    Your wine is tasteless, pleasureless your ease ;
Behind your brutal talk you are cold and lonely,
    Sick of the laughter of such men as these.

And even they at times perceive you moody,
    Bid you cheer up, are vaguely tired of you,
Damper of pleasure, hypocrite, prig, superior,
    Too cranky and vain to think as others do.

For, suddenly, your answers grow abstracted,
    Empty, or rough ; your eyes go over sea,
Watching a distant sail that seems unmoving,
    The symbol of some lost tranquillity :

A silent sail that cuts the clear horizon,
    A warm blue sea, a tranquil, cloudless sky,
You sit and gaze, and, as you stare, they guess you
    Indifferent though the whole of them should die.

III

'The poet should be chaste, his verses——' well,
  It wasn't Lesbia's view, she did her best,
Tempting and spurning, to weary and degrade you,
  To callous you and make you like the rest.

Disliking, piqued by, that strange difference in you,
  Contemptuous and curious, she would dare
And then deny, provoke and then repel you,
  Yet could not make you other than you were.

The soft-pressed foot, the glance that hinted heat,
  The scanty favours always auguring more,
The haughty, cold indifference, mingling twin
  Frigidities of the vestal and the whore,

Still could not even more than wound, cloud over,
  The eager boy in you she so despised,
The love of fineness, sweetness, loyalty, candour,
  The innocent country memories you prized.

IV

A flower in a garden grew, Catullus,
  Some time you saw it, and the memory stayed.
One flower of all the flowers you ever glanced at,
  A perfect thing of dew and radiance made :

Emblem of youth, plucked, carried away and droop-
     ing,
  Out of the garden ; emblem of your lot,
Perplexed, bewildered, languishing, an alien
  Who was born to cherish all his world forgot.

117

A GOODBYE FROM THE SHIP

MEETINGS are only partings, friend.
We might have known
That in the end
Every one goes on his way alone . . .
We shared blue mornings on the sea,
White mountain-moons.
You played for me
On your bamboo-flute the Chinese tunes
That went with wine-cups and the song
Chrysanthemum sang,
Ten stanzas long,
When she laughed with us in Chinkiang.
Pure were the poems you explained
On Canton walls
The day it rained ;
And always now the twilight falls
More quietly because you said :
' This is the hour
When griefs are shed
As light as petals from a flower.'
These things and other things are mine
To bless you for.
We send a sign
Of goodwill, between ship and shore . . .
Meetings like ours have always shone
Beyond their end—
But we might have known
Meetings are only partings, friend.

GERALD GOULD

COMPENSATION

HERE, in the field, last year,
　I saw a seagull die,
Flying inland, for fear
　Of change in the sky.

Seagulls six and seven
　Flew inland, and cried :
And one fell out of Heaven
　Here, and died.

I found no scar or stain :
　He was white and grey, like smoke.
He flew, and was in pain,
　And his heart broke.

Now, when I come this way,
　I remember his beauty and pride,
And how from the hollow of day
　He fell, and died.

Then, I too was proud ;
　I was angry to see death.
The hour, that was warm and loud,
　Drew one cold breath.

Again the gulls are flying.
　My heart, that then was a lover
Hot and high, is dying—
　But the gulls fly over.

AMY LOWELL

ORIENTATION

WHEN the young ladies of the boarding-school
    take the air
They walk in pairs, each holding a blush-red parasol
    against the sun.
From my window they look like an ambulating
    parterre
Of roses, I cannot tell one from one.

There is a certain young person I dream of by night
And paint by day on little two-by-three inch squares
Of ivory. Which is she ? Which of all the parasols in
    sight
Covers the blithe, mocking face which stares
At me from twenty miniatures, confusing the single-
    ness of my delight ?

You know my window well enough—the fourth
    from the corner. Oh, you know.
Slant your parasol a bit this way, if you please,
And take for yourself the very correct bow
I make toward the line of demure young ladies
Perambulating the street in a neat row.
It is true I have never seen beneath your parasol,
Therefore my miniatures resemble one another not
    at all.

You must pick yourself like a button-hole bouquet,
And lift the parasol to my face one day,
And let me see you laughing at the sun—
Or at me. Then I will choose the one
Of my twenty miniatures most like you
And destroy the others, with which I shall have
      nothing more to do.

A. NEWBERRY CHOYCE

LET ME LOVE BRIGHT THINGS

LET me love bright things
  Before my life is over . . .
Moons, and shining wings
  Of bees about the clover.

Bathers in seas;
  Cities by night;
Tall rainy trees;
  Yellow candle-light.

And long sunlit lands
  That lie anywhere;
And one with white hands
  To comb her gleaming hair!

B. WORSLEY-GOUGH

GRATITUDE

ENGLAND, of all the debts we owe to thee
For gifts unnumbered to thy humblest sons—
Sunshine, and laughter, and the wind that runs—
To wake the world at dawn, and every tree
Standing alone in grave tranquillity ;
Swift streams, and the great hills that gave them
    birth,
And the glad fragrance of the rain-washed earth—
We owe thee most for these in memory.

So, when we are alone in other lands,
And dream of all the glory we have known
And left behind, each dear, familiar scene
Is ours again. The strong and tender hands
Of England hold us, and her songs are blown
About us, bridging all the seas between.

LOUIS UNTERMEYER

WATERS OF BABYLON

WHAT presses about us here in the evening
　　As you open a window and stare at a stone gray
　　　　sky,
And the streets give back the jangle of meaningless
　　　　movement
That is tired of life and almost too tired to die.

Night comes on, and even the night is wounded ;
　　There, on its breast, it carries a curved, white scar.
What will you find out there that is not torn and
　　　　anguished ?
　　Can God be less distressed than the least of His
　　　　creatures are ?

Below are the blatant lights in a huddled squalor ;
　　Above are futile fires in a freezing space.
What can they give that you should look to them for
　　　　compassion
　　Though you bare your heart and lift an im-
　　　　ploring face ?

They have seen, by countless waters and windows,
　　The women of your race facing a stony sky ;
They have heard, for thousands of years, the voices
　　　　of women
　　Asking them : 'Why . . .?'

Let the night be : it has neither knowledge nor pity.
One thing alone can hope to answer your fear ;
It is that which struggles and blinds us and burns
between us. . . .
Let the night be. Close the window, belovèd.
. . . Come here.

JOHN GOULD FLETCHER

BLUE WATER

SEA-VIOLINS are playing on the sands ;
Curved bows of blue and white are flying over
    the pebbles,
See them attack the chords—dark basses, glinting
    trebles.
Dimly and faint they croon, blue violins.
'Suffer without regret,' they seem to cry,
'Though dark your suffering is, it may be music,
Waves of blue heat that wash midsummer sky :
Sea-violins that play along the sands.'

EDITH SITWELL

PROMENADE SENTIMENTALE

(Professor Goose-Cap speaks)

ONE time when the cold red winter sun,
Like a Punch-and-Judy show shrilled in fun,

And scattered down its green perfume
Like the dust that drifts from the green lime-bloom,

I sat at my dressing-table (that chilly
Palely crinolined water-lily),

And watched my face as spired and brittle
As the tall fish tangled in a little

Dark weed, that sea-captains keep
In bottles and perpetual sleep.

My face seemed the King of Spain's dry map,
All seared with gold—no one cared a rap

When I walked on the grass like the sheepish buds
Of wool that grow on lambs chewing their cuds.

The small flowers grew to a hairy husk
That holds Eternity for musk,

And the satyr's daughter came : I saw
She was golden as Venus' castle of straw,

And the curls round her golden fruit-face shine
Like black ivy berries that will not make wine.

Like my black cloak (a three-tiered ship on the Main),
And my face like the map of the King of Spain.

Beneath the boughs when like ragged goose-plumes
Of the snow hang the Spring's first chilly blooms,

I swept on towards her ; my foot with the gout
Clattered like satyr-hoofs, put her to rout,

For she thought that I was the satyr king,
So she fled like the uncouth wind of Spring

Across the sea that was green as grass,
Where bird-soft archipelagos pass,

To where like golden bouquets lay
Asia, Africa, and Cathay.

And now the bird-soft light and shade
Touches me not : I promenade

Where rain falls with tinkling notes and cold,
Like the castanet sound of the thinnest gold

In chess-board gardens where, knight and pawn
Of ivory, scentless flowers are born.

MILDRED PLEW MERRYMAN

TO CHICAGO AT NIGHT

SPUTTER, city ! Bead with fire
Every ragged roof and spire ;

Splash your brilliance on the sky
Till you blind the moon's round eye ;

Let your jagged branding mark
Scorch across the velvet dark

Till the night beneath your sting
Shrivels like a crumpling wing.

Burst to bloom, you proud, white flower,
But remember—that hot hour

When the shadow of your brand
Laps the last cool grain of sand—

You will still be just a scar
On a little, lonesome star.

ROBERT GRAVES

MIRROR, MIRROR

MIRROR, mirror, tell me,
  Am I pretty or plain?
Or am I downright ugly,
  And ugly to remain?

Shall I marry a gentleman?
  Shall I marry a clown?
Or shall I marry old knives-and-scissors
  Shouting through the town?

HENRY BELLAMANN

HOME-SICKNESS

THERE is a land so far away,
Almost it seems never to have been.
There are dull rocks
And the brown flanks of barren hills.
There is a listless stream
Waits in the shallows,
Nor desires the sea.

Old walls are rooted deep,
And gaunt houses sit upon their haunches
Like starved animals ;
Sometimes their hollow windows
Show a wolfish gleam
In the heavy dark.

But I am kin to it.
The old-wife hills,
I am close kin to them.

Here the cloudy light
Circles on crystalline peaks,
And the soft fall of satin petals
Stirs wide eddies of perfume
In the emerald pools
Of walled gardens.

Here the delicate accent
Of bright waters
And the cadenced music
Of a gentle tongue
Float upon the air
And curl themselves in silence
As late sunlight
Fades in deep rivers.

The grapes have purpled many times
Against that wall.
I know the fountain's legend now
By heart ;
The story of this gracious land
Is told.

Those harsh, time-eaten hills,
Like peasant women, stooped and shawled,
They crouch as though to warm themselves together :
They wait, as peasant women wait,
For their own sons.

I must go back to them ;
I must go back.

SYLVIA LYND

FAREWELL IN FEBRUARY

I

THROUGH the small window on the stair
    As I leant out to take the air
At the slow-fading end of day,
I heard the thrushes sing and say:
This is the end of winter.

This is the end, I thought, although
The northward fields are rimmed with snow,
And like a thrush's breast the down
Is speckled o'er with white and brown;
Though no sharp plough the furrow grooves,
Though still the seagulls' white-winged droves
Flurry above the inland plain—
Winter withdraws from earth again—
This is the end of winter.

Since then, I thought, I shall not see
New buds alight in every tree,
Nor watch the sun at evenfall
Put gold upon my bedroom wall,
And no more at this window lean
To feel the sweet air pressing in—
Here for a little while I'll rest
And mark the garden's every crest,
That in my mind when I am gone
Its birds and boughs may still live on.

II

This place that I'll not see again
Shall wear its seasons in my brain;
Clothed in fine weather it shall shine
Through what journeys may be mine;
Nor drought nor deluge shall destroy
What in my fancy I enjoy.
Here not a seed on barren ground
Shall fall, and not a grub be found.
All happy weathers, seasons, hours,
Entangled still with fruit and flowers,
In gay confusion shall display
The charms of Michaelmas or May.
Fresh leaves and blossoms I'll set in it
And plums shall ripened be next minute;
Though scarlet currants that appear
Like earrings in a lady's ear
Shall slant the beams of morning sun—
Next pinks breathe sweet and day be done:
There be the moon and there tiptoe
The stars among the branches go,
And that young jasmine by the wall
Shall grow a flowery waterfall.
So rich in crops, so quickly weeded,
Where never fork or hoe is needed,
This place I leave beneath grey skies
Shall be my spirit's paradise.

III

What once was there and what there never,
Who from thought's thicket can dissever ?
Through the green branches looking down
Into this Eden of my own,
Unchanging phantoms I shall see
Myself and you who walked with me,
Two skipping children long since grown,
A cat long dead and birds long flown,
And so substantial I shall find
The dreams that living leaves behind,
All hopes, all loves, all ecstasies
Stolen from life, I shall find these.
What memory cannot paint be sure
Fancy will fashion more secure.

Those woven boughs, that silken sky,
Regret nor winter will come nigh ;
Beyond the reach of mortal grief
Its every shining flower and leaf ;
Growing but fading not shall be
The span of its mortality,
And time's sad progress shall be stayed
By the perfection of a shade.

ELINOR WYLIE

QUARREL

LET us quarrel for these reasons :
You detest the salt which seasons
My speech ; and all my lights go out
In the cold poison of your doubt.
I love Shelley, you love Keats ;
Something parts and something meets.
I love salads, you love chops ;
Something starts and something stops ;
Something hides its face and cries ;
Something shivers ; something dies.
I love blue ribbons brought from fairs ;
You love sitting splitting hairs.
I love truth, and so do you.
Tell me, is it truly true ?

BLANCHE SHOEMAKER WAGSTAFF

WILDNESS

LOVE forged for me a golden chain
To bind my straying feet.
I dwelt in scented rose-leaf rain
And found the young years sweet.

But when I hear the wind sweep by
Or see the white clouds pass—
The spaces of the open sky—
Birds soaring o'er the grass—

There is a little place in me
That cries like any child
To be as forest things are, free,
Lonely, and strange and wild !

V. SACKVILLE-WEST

WINTER SONG

MANY have sung the summer's songs,
Many have sung the corn ;
Many have sung white blossom too
That stars the naked thorn—
That stars the black and naked thorn
Against the chalky blue.

But I, crouched up beside the hearth,
Will sing the red and grey ;
Red going-down of sun behind
Clubbed woods of winter's day ;
Of winter's short and hodden day
That seals the sober hind ;

Seals him sagacious through the year
Since winter comes again ;
Since harvest's but another toil,
And sorrow through the grain
Mounts up, through swathes of ripest grain,
The sorrow of the soil.

No lightness is there at their heart,
No joy in country folk ;
Only a patience slow and grave
Beneath their labours' yoke—
Beneath the earth's compelling yoke
That only serves its slave.

138

The countryman for ever holds
The winter's memory,
When he, before the planets' fires
Have faded from the sky,
From black, resplendent winter sky,
Must go about his byres;

And whether to the reapers' whirr
That scythes the falling crops,
He travels round the widening wake
Between the corn and copse,
The stubble wake 'twixt corn and copse
Where gleaners ply the rake,

Or whether in his granary loft
He pours the winnowed sacks,
Or whether in his yard he routs
The vermin from the stacks—
The vermin from the staddled stacks
With staves and stones and shouts,

Still, still through all the molten eves,
Whether he reaps or hones,
Or counts the guerdon of his sweat,
Still to his inward bones,
His ancient, sage, sardonic bones—
The winter haunts him yet.

Winter and toil reward him still
While he his course shall go
According to his proven worth,
Until his faith shall know
The ultimate justice, and the slow
Compassion of the earth.

FRANCES CHESTERTON

HOW FAR IS IT TO BETHLEHEM?

HOW far is it to Bethlehem?
  Not very far.
Shall we find the stable-room
  Lit by a star?

Can we see the little Child,
  Is He within?
If we lift the wooden latch
  May we go in?

May we stroke the creatures there,
  Ox, ass, or sheep?
May we peep like them and see
  Jesus asleep?

If we touch His tiny hand
  Will He awake?
Will He know we've come so far
  Just for His sake?

Great Kings have precious gifts,
  And we have naught;
Little smiles and little tears
  Are all we brought.

For all weary children
    Mary must weep.
Here, on His bed of straw,
    Sleep, children, sleep.

God, in His Mother's arms,
    Babes in the byre,
Sleep, as they sleep who find
    Their heart's desire.

R. L. GALES

THE HAPPY NIGHT

IN the hard winter of the world
A sudden summer now is seen ;
At Grenoble the walnut trees
Bedeck themselves with fragrant green.

.   .   .   .   .

To-night there are no walls of fire
Around the Cave of Heart's Desire,
But kind the midnight is and gay
That bears the bud of Easter Day.
It weaves a rustic, homely spell,
The music of an old vielle ;
Its humdrum sweetness seems to-night
Adventurous and infinite,
The Prelude played in lowly wise
To things hid from the Angels' eyes.
The air is filled with tinkling chimes,
The blessing of all happy times :
All spirits know an influence blent
Of awe and wonder with content ;
Suzanne her fireside bellows plies
To the high Gloria of the skies.
The earth feels streaming near and far
Long rays of some benignant star ;
Now even as the shepherds pipe
On distant hills the grapes are ripe.

.   .   .   .

At Grenoble the walnut trees
Bedeck themselves with fragrant green ;
In the hard winter of the world
A sudden summer now is seen.

LAURENCE HOUSMAN

A CHRISTMAS CAROL

WHEN Love on Earth set up His rest,
　Within a safe and secret place,
His stronghold was a Virgin's breast,
　His light her stooping face.
　　Then oped the Everlasting bars,
　　　Then sky-bells rung ;
　　And all the lovers of the stars
　　　Came down and sung !

For since Love may not dwell alone,
　Around Him, in attendant train,
Those flaming fires which formed His throne
　Fell down to Earth like rain.
　　O happy, happy falling fires,
　　　That from your height,
　　Unto a world of blind desires
　　　Bring gift of sight !

The Word goes forth, and with Him drawn,
　Hark, in unending voice of song,
The birds of God's celestial dawn
　Sing, to sing out man's wrong !
　　O happy, happy birds of night,
　　　That from your rest
　　Swoop down, and from the fields of light
　　　Make Earth your nest !

Around the Stable shone that light,
  Within the stall that song was heard ;
But showed not there as stars to sight,
  Nor sang like voice of bird :
    The sound—a Maiden's heaving heart,
      All full of grace ;
    The light, of Heaven's dawns a part,
      Her stooping face !